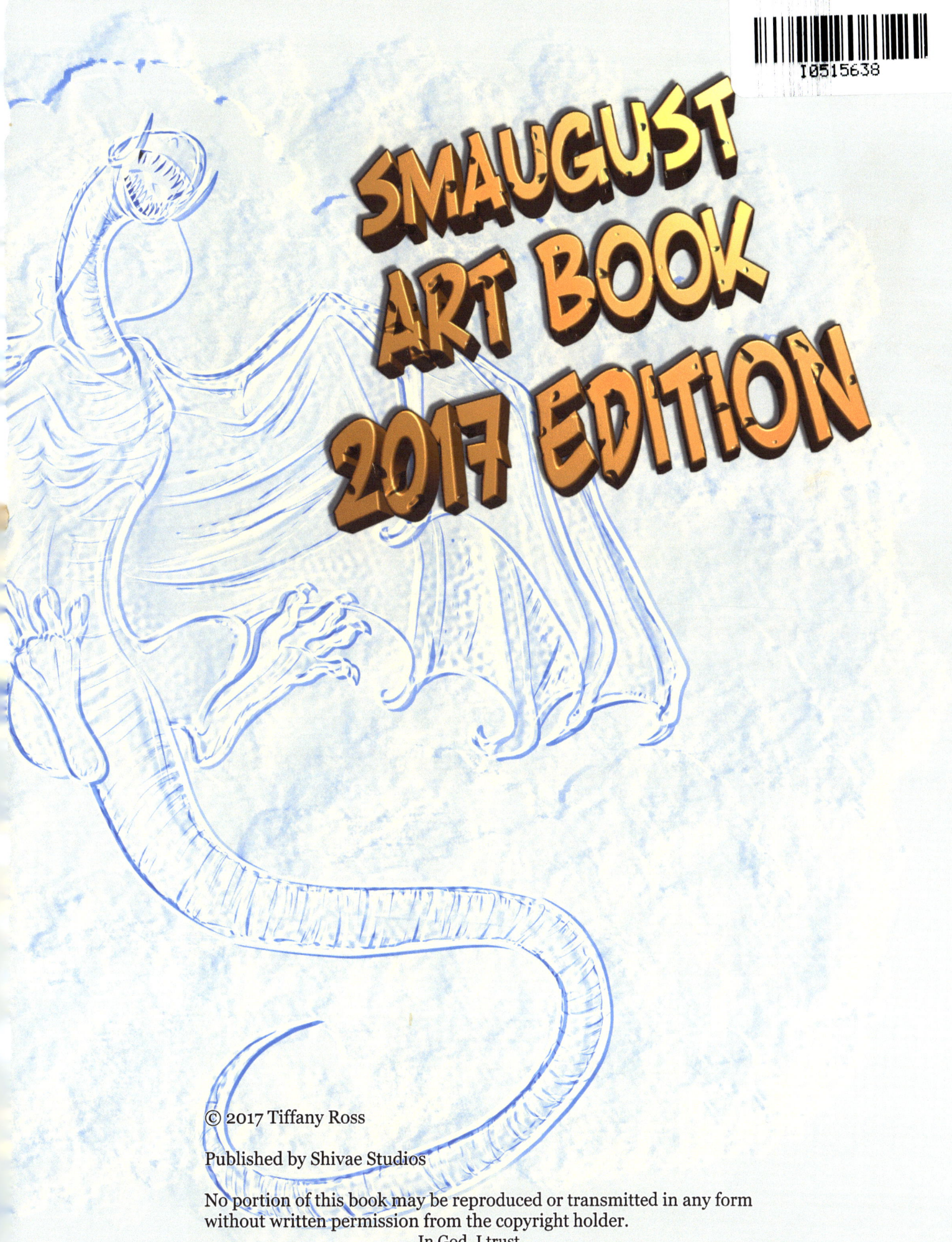

SMAUGUST ART BOOK 2017 EDITION

© 2017 Tiffany Ross

Published by Shivae Studios

No portion of this book may be reproduced or transmitted in any form without written permission from the copyright holder.
In God, I trust.

#SMAUGUST
DRAWING CHALLENGE
31 DAYS OF DRAGONS!

1. RED DRAGON
2. BABY DRAGON
3. DRAGON RIDER
4. PET DRAGON
5. UNDERWATER DRAGON
6. GAME OF THRONES INSPIRED DRAGON
7. FURRY DRAGON
8. DRAGON AND A KNIGHT
9. FOREST DRAGON
10. BLUE DRAGON
11. HYDRA
12. VOLCANIC DRAGON
13. ICE DRAGON
14. FEATHERED DRAGON
15. DESERT DRAGON
16. DRAGON GUARDING ITS HOARD
17. CHINESE DRAGON
18. ROYAL DRAGON
19. LIGHTNING DRAGON
20. A WYVERN
21. MINIATURE DRAGON
22. FAIRY DRAGON
23. CRYSTAL DRAGON
24. TWO HEADED DRAGON
25. BONE DRAGON
26. DRAGONS IN LOVE
27. ANTHRO DRAGON
28. HORNED DRAGON
29. DRAGON IN FLIGHT
30. CUTE DRAGON
31. SMAUG

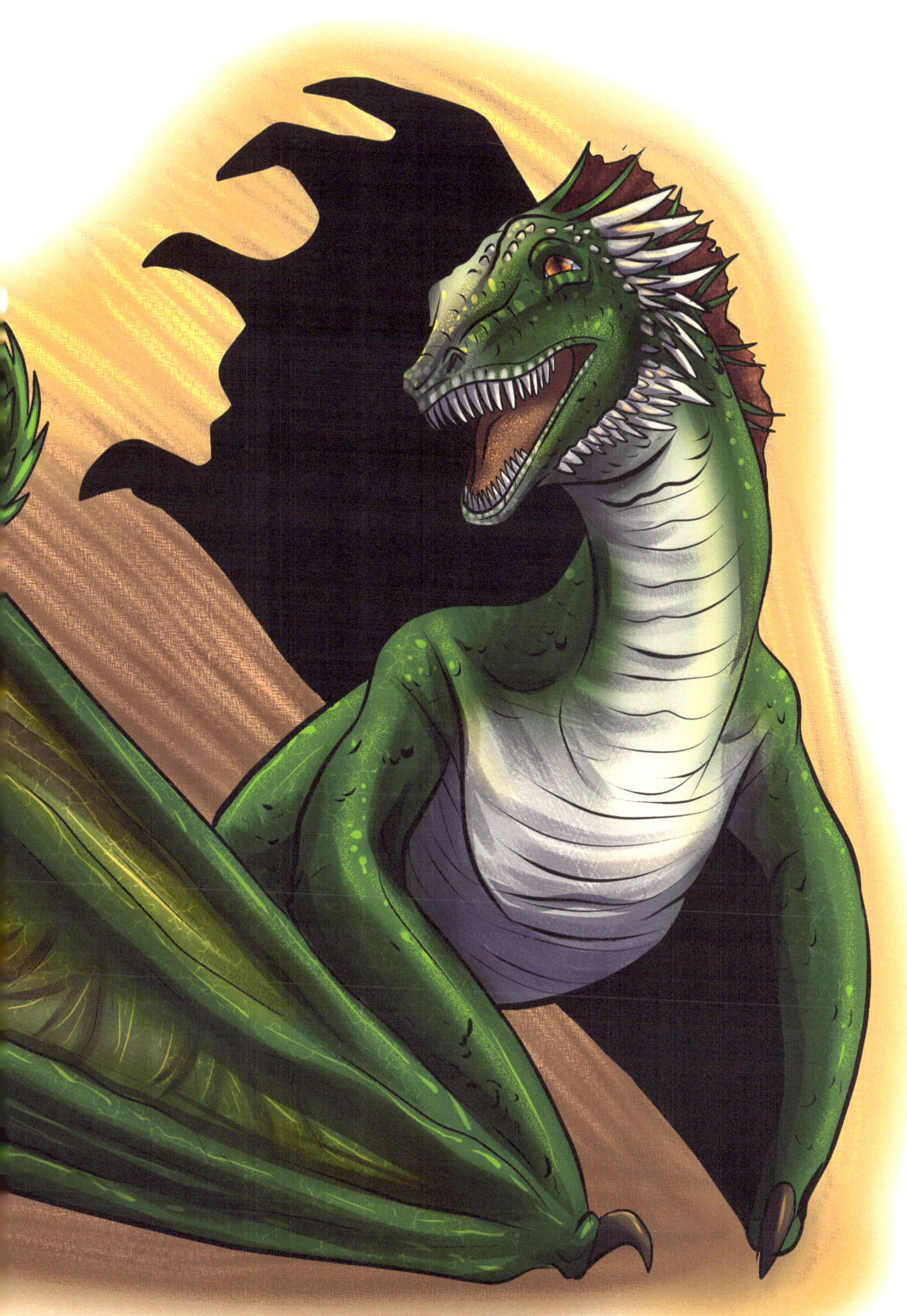

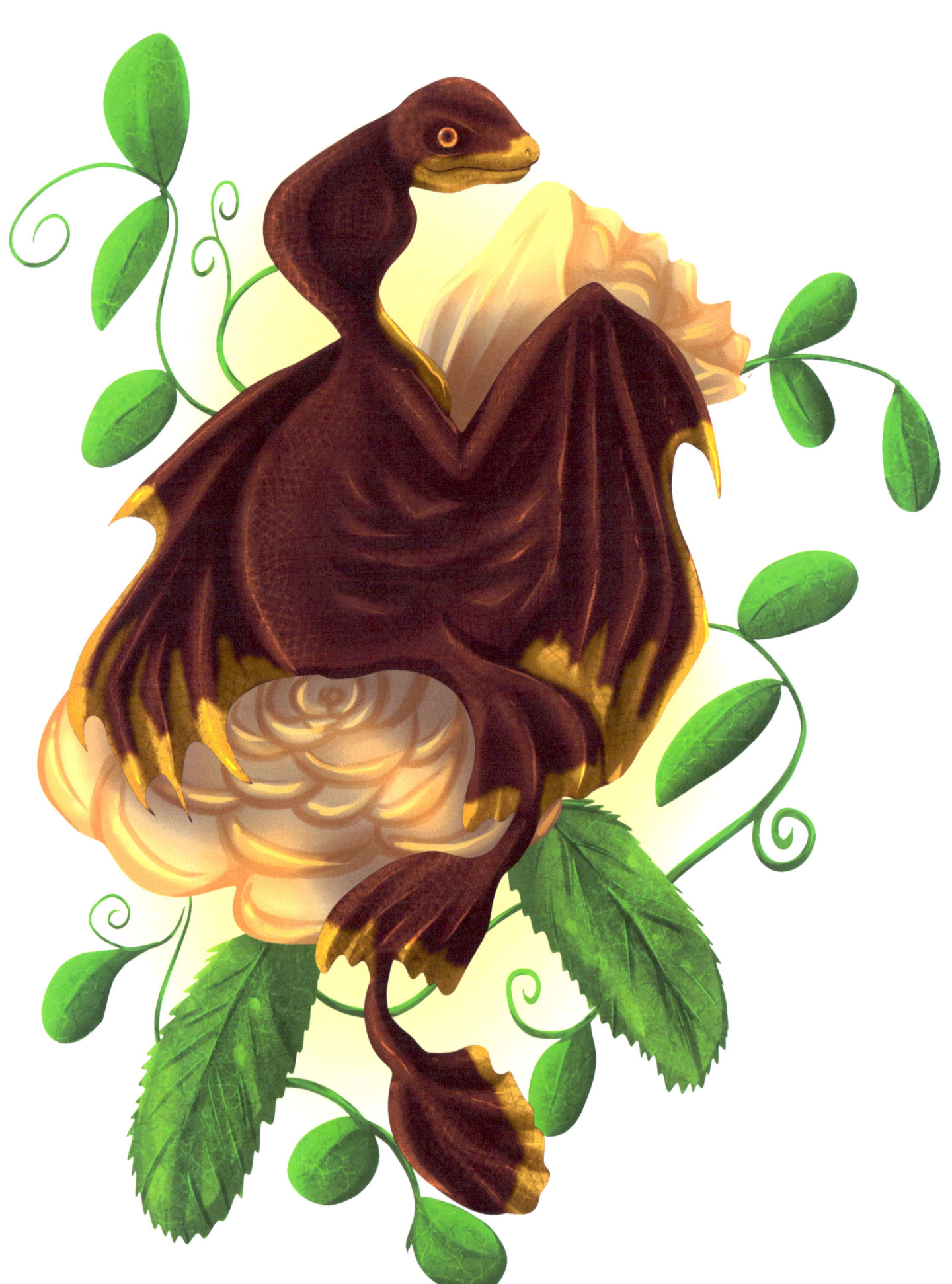

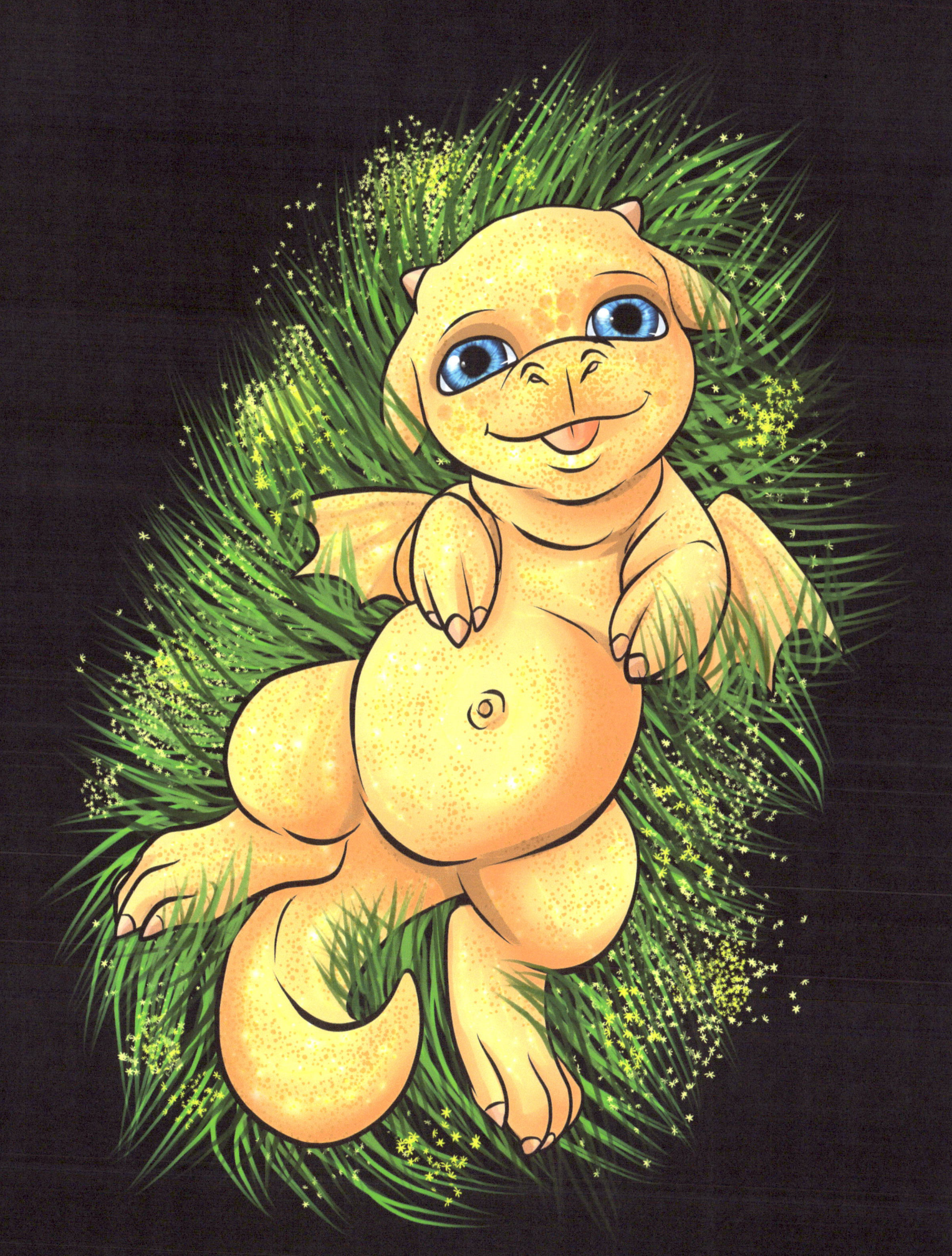

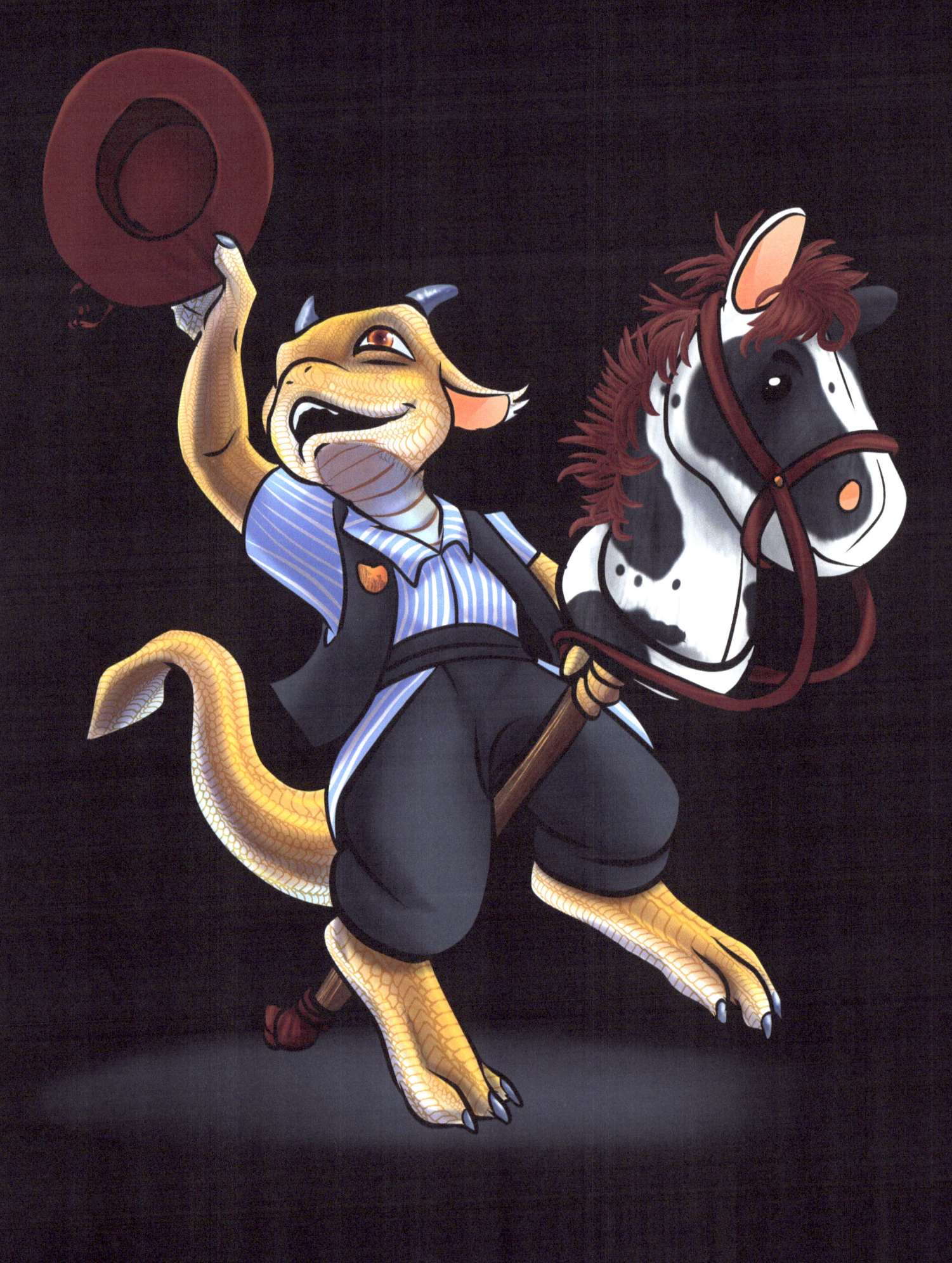

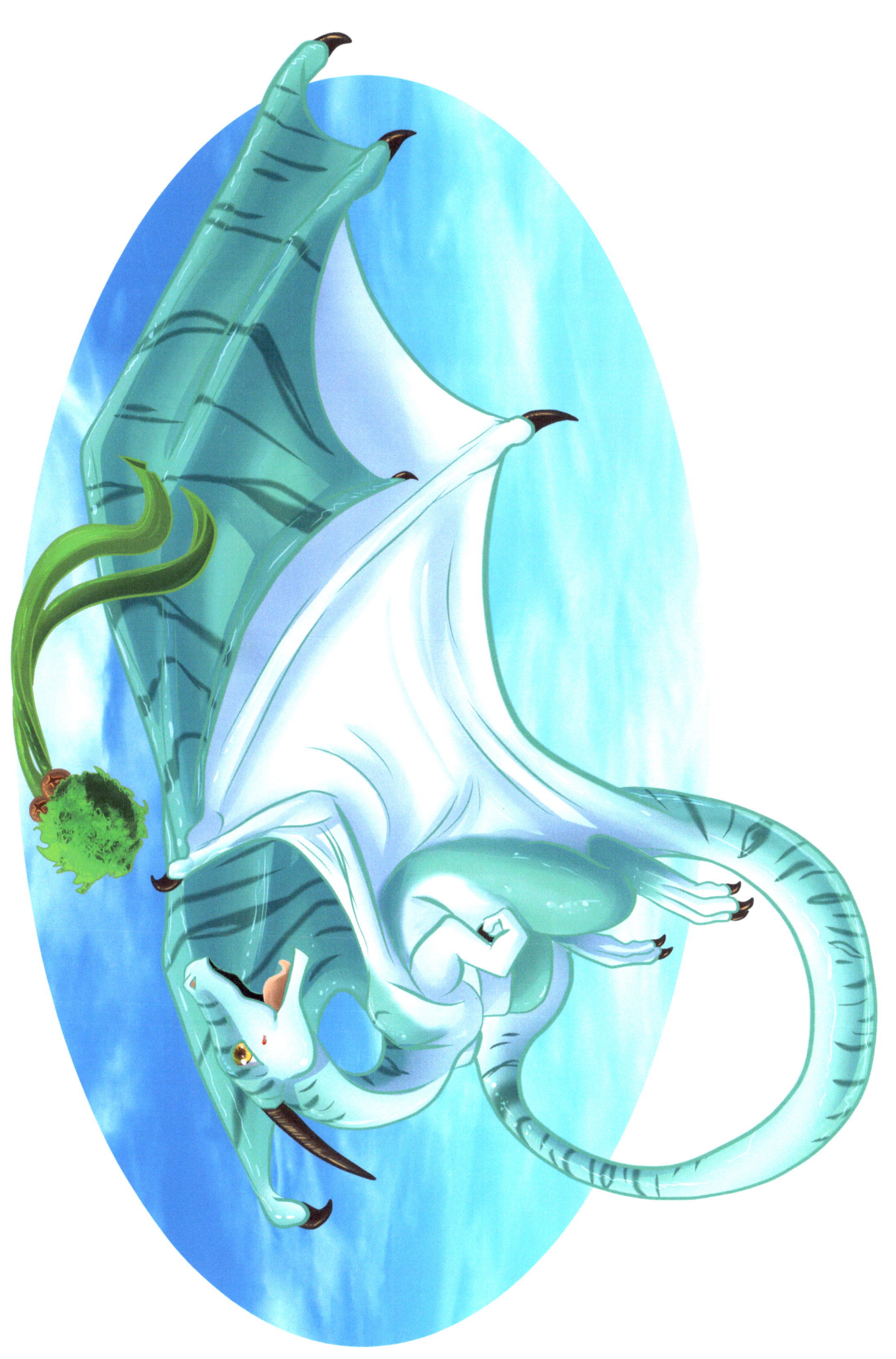

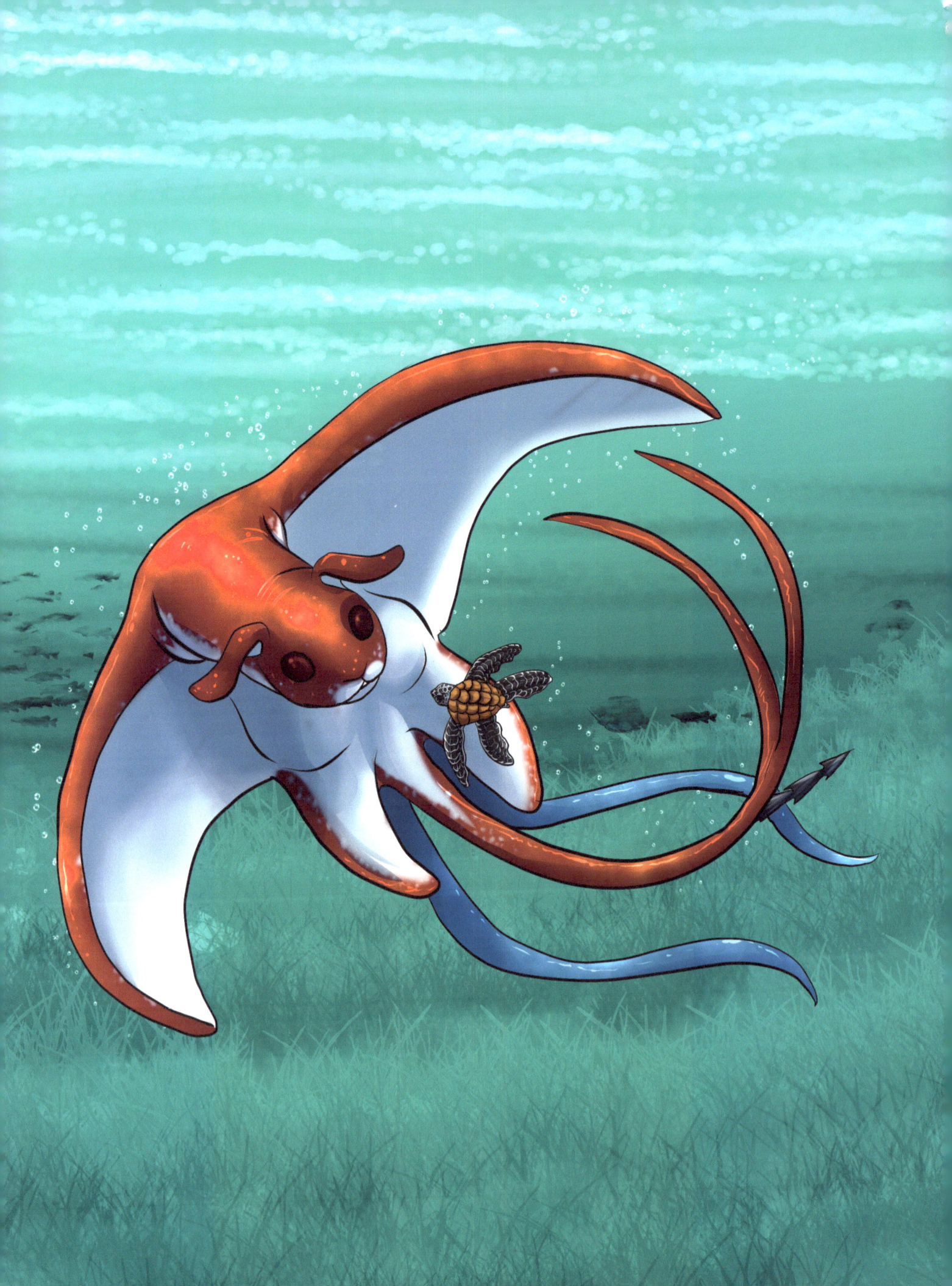

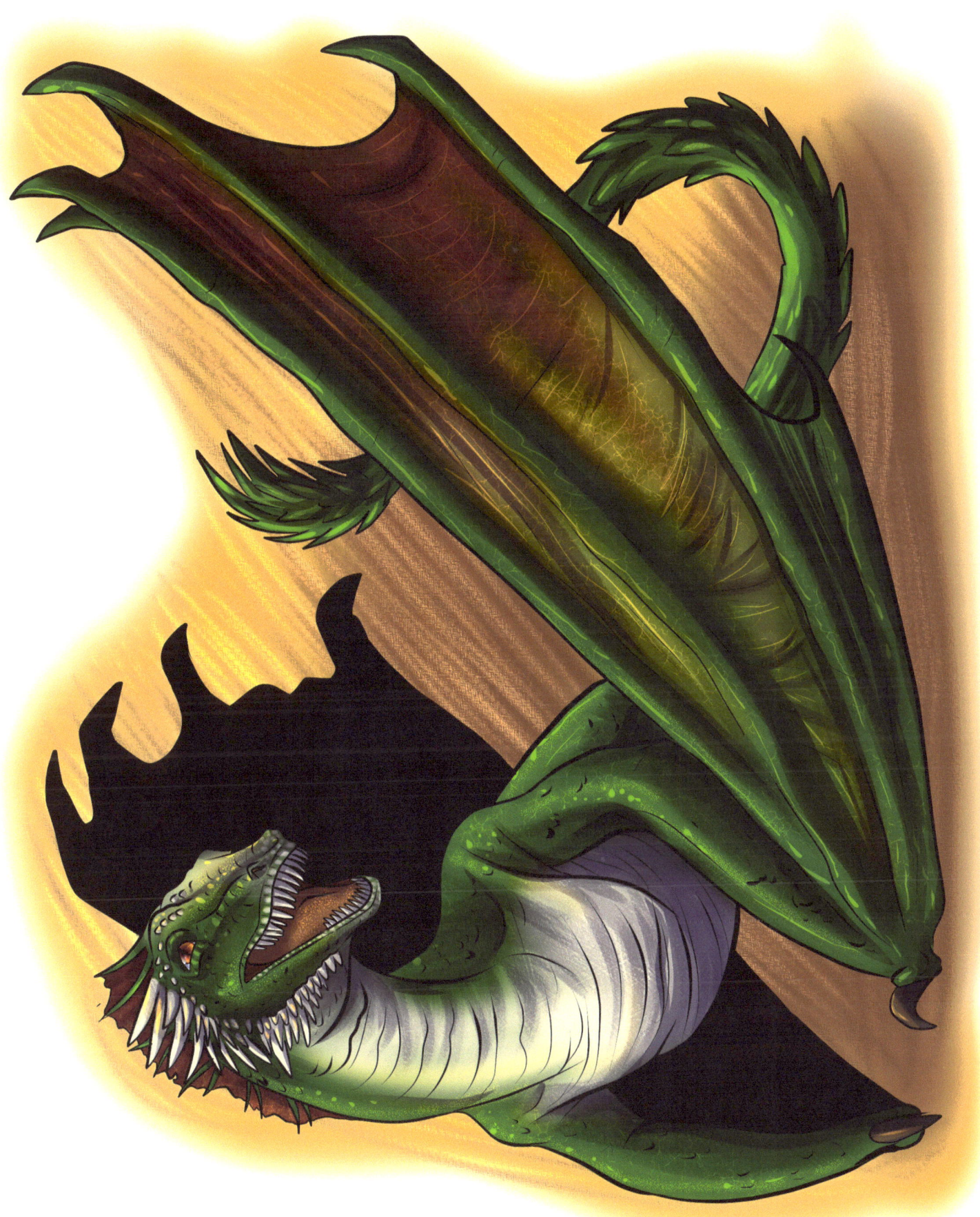

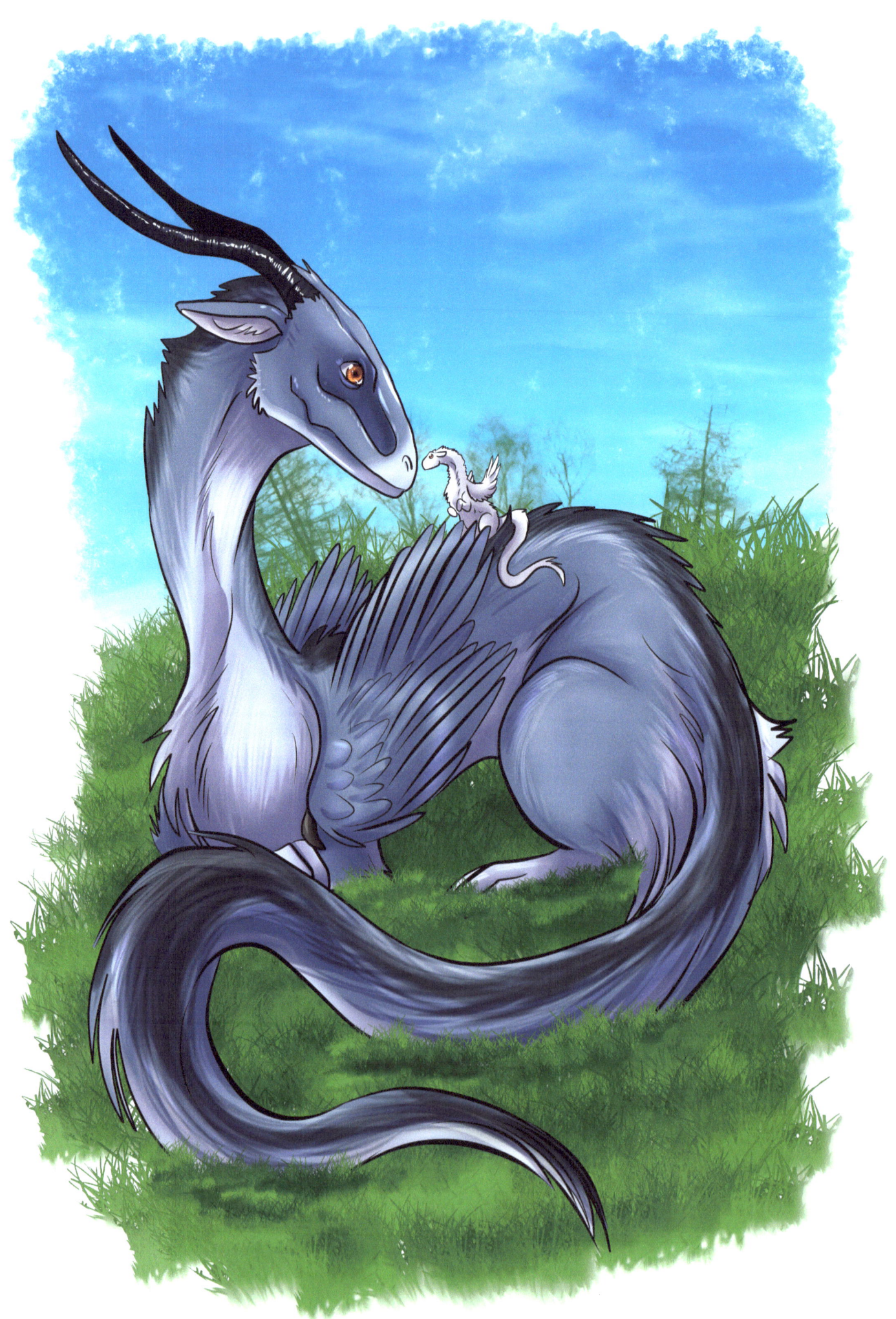

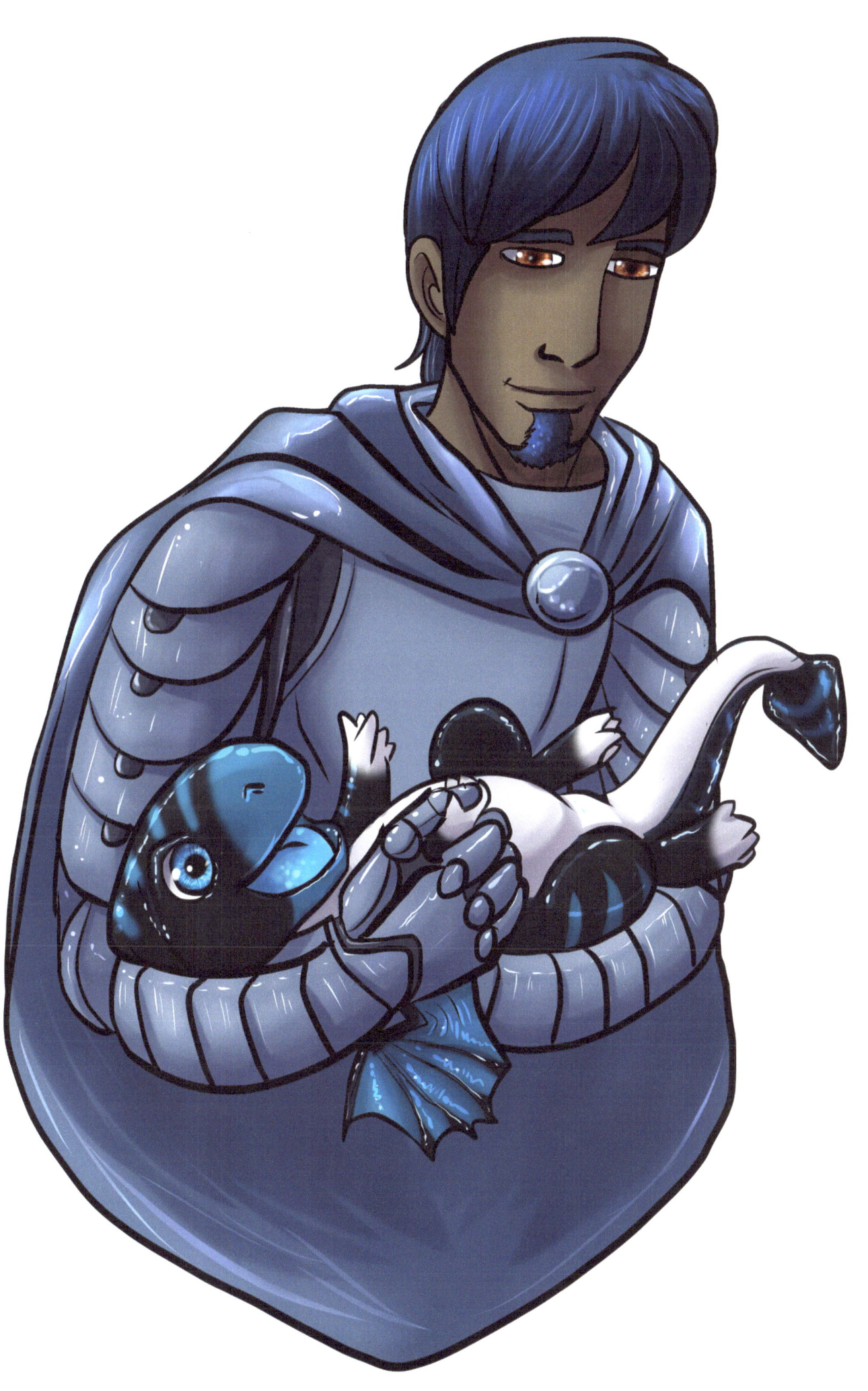

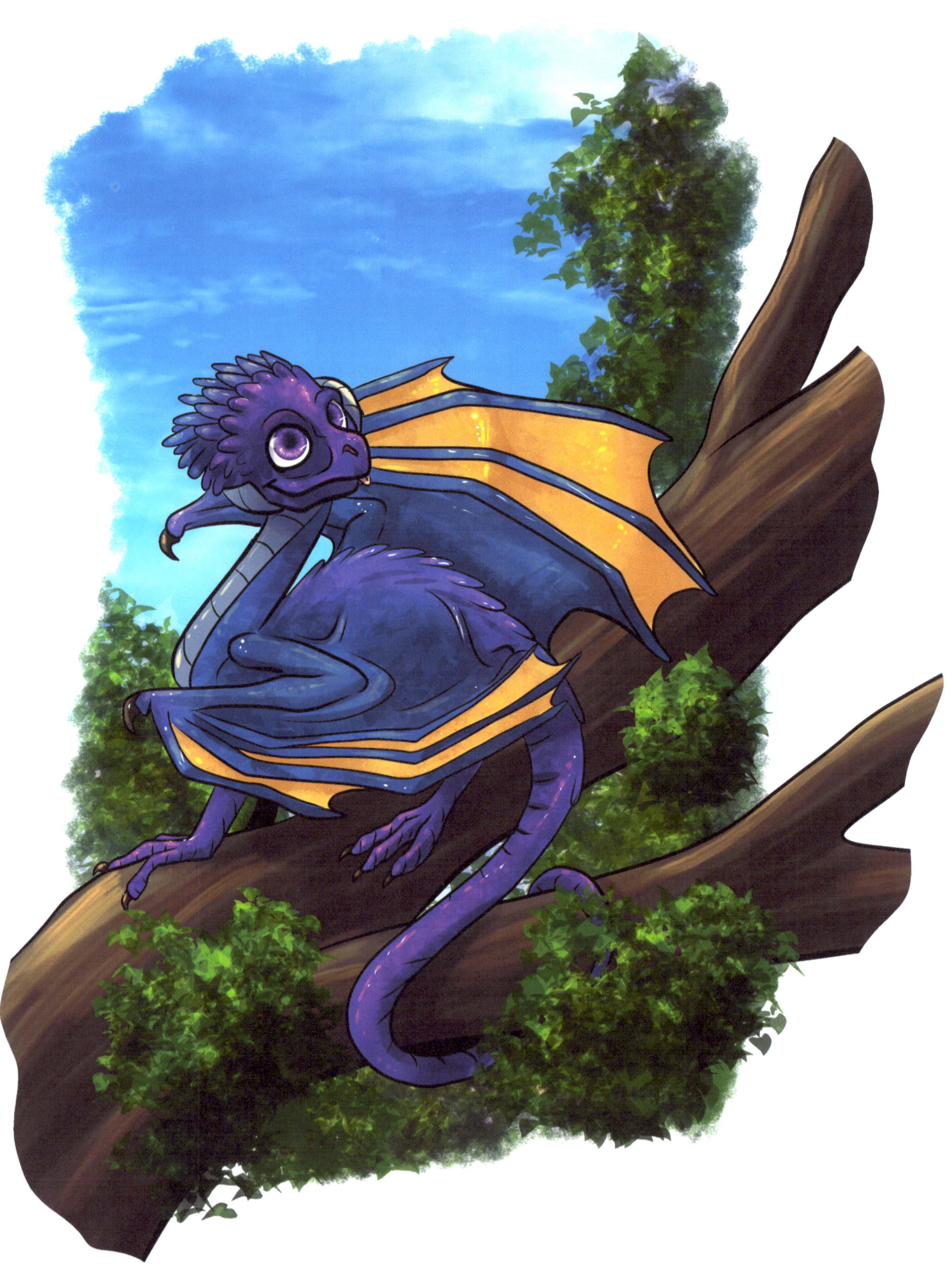

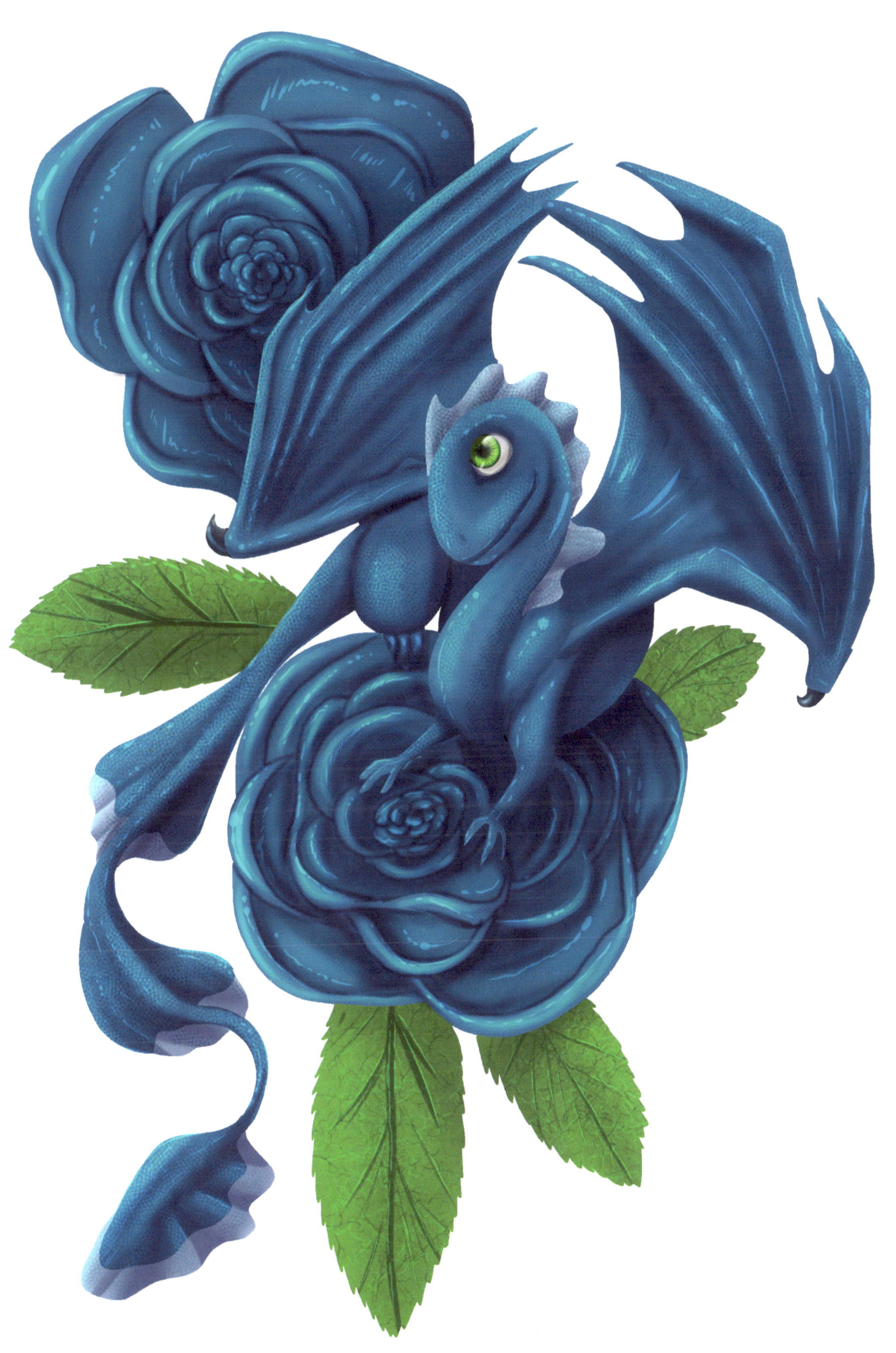

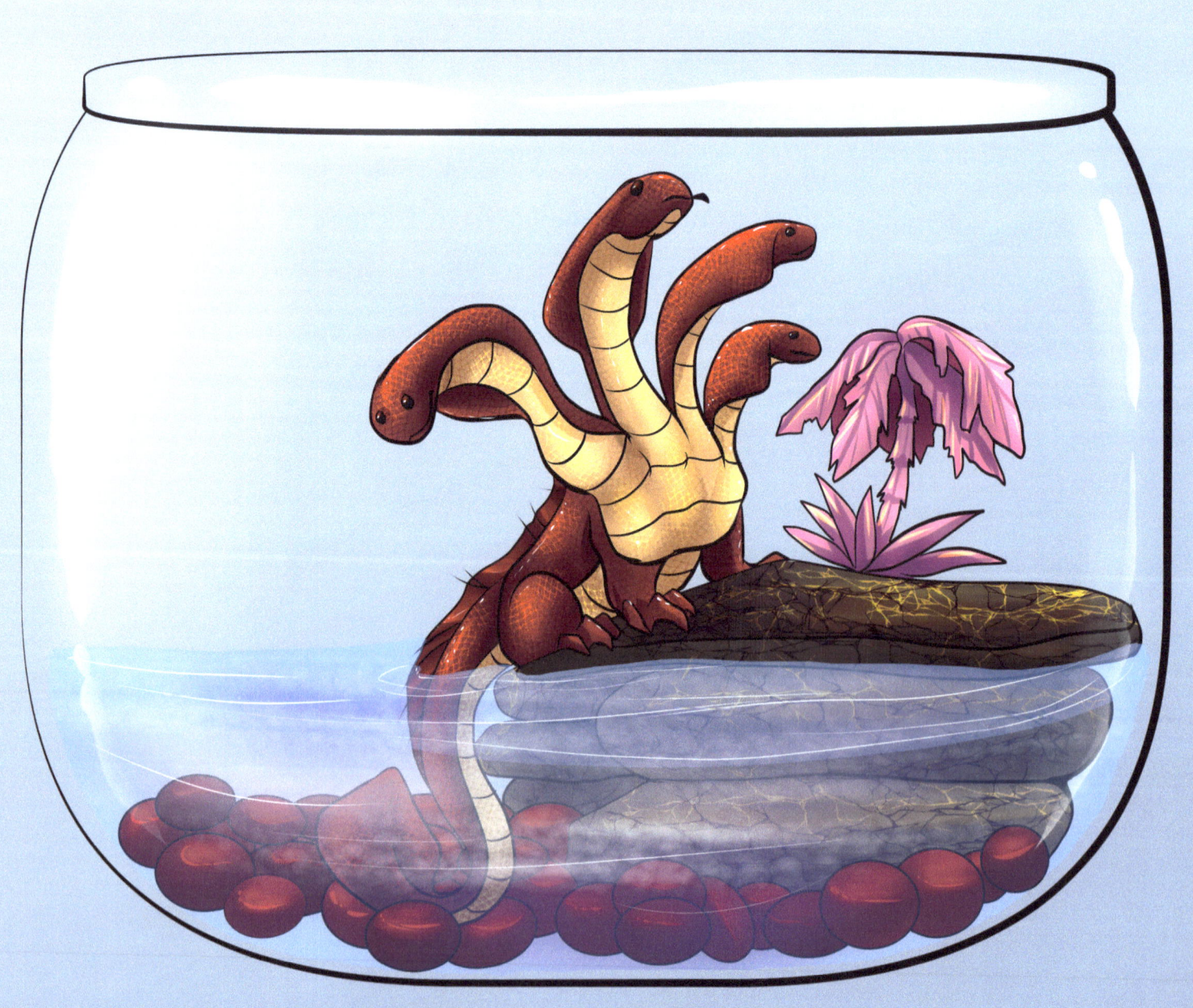

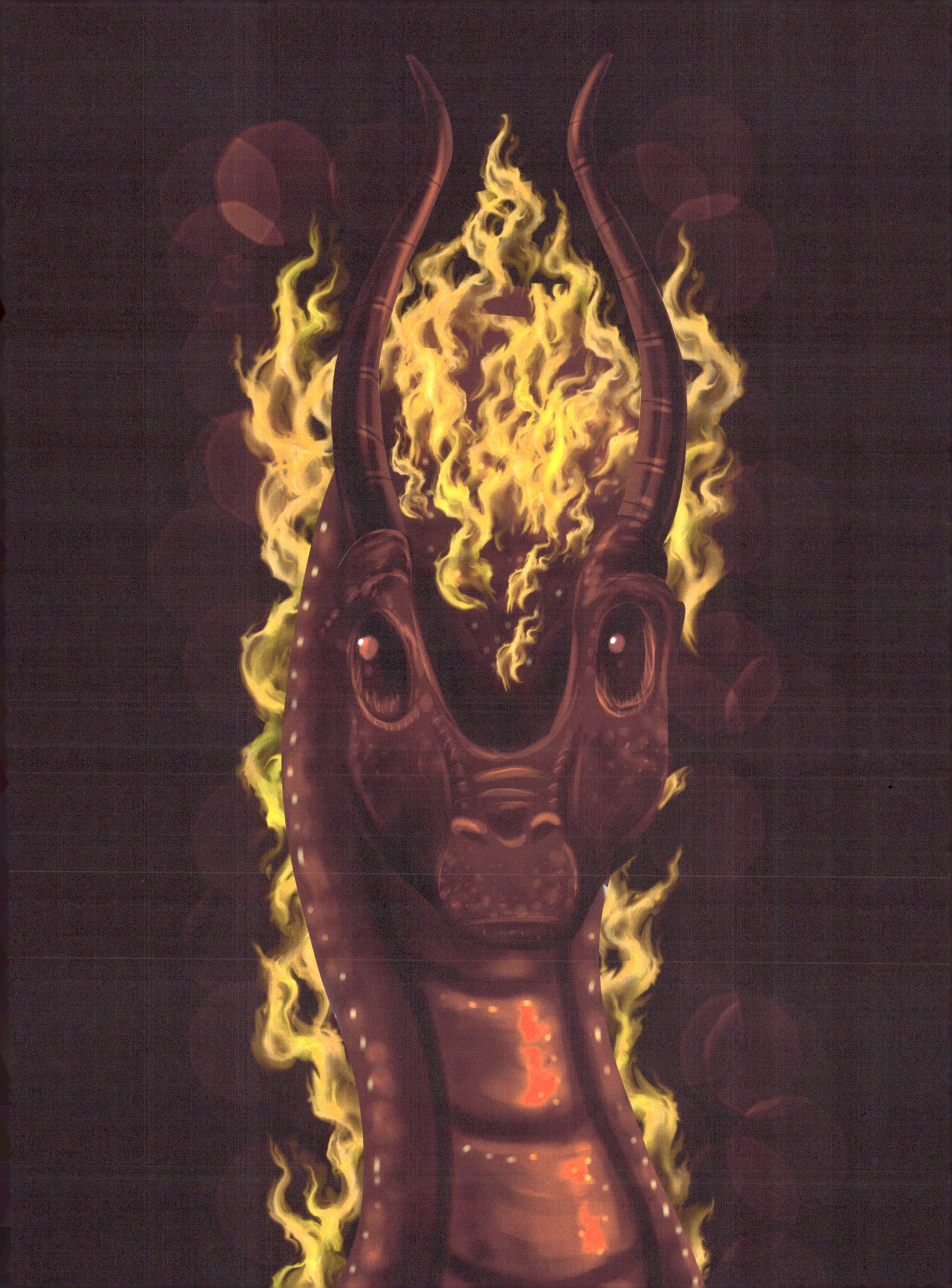

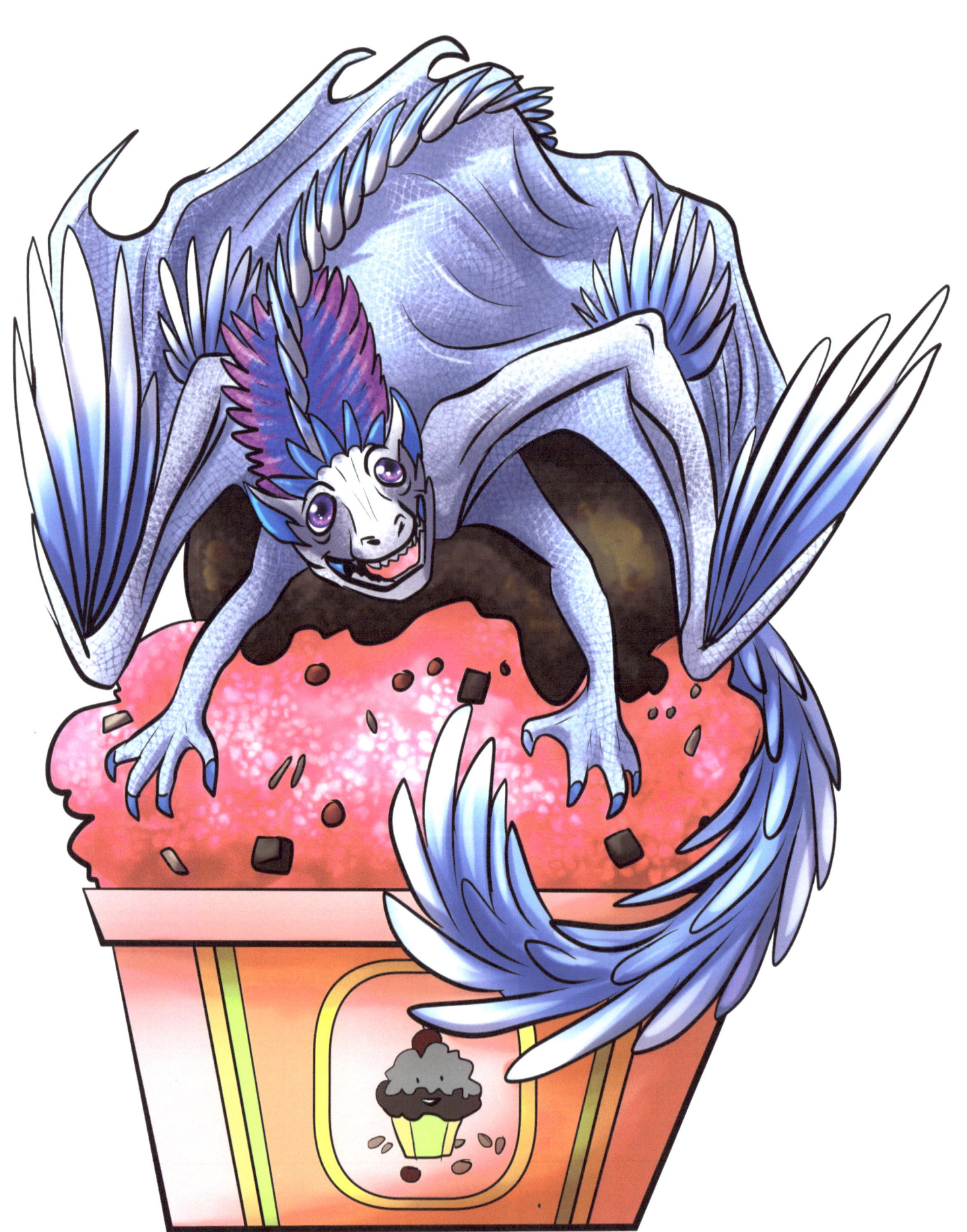

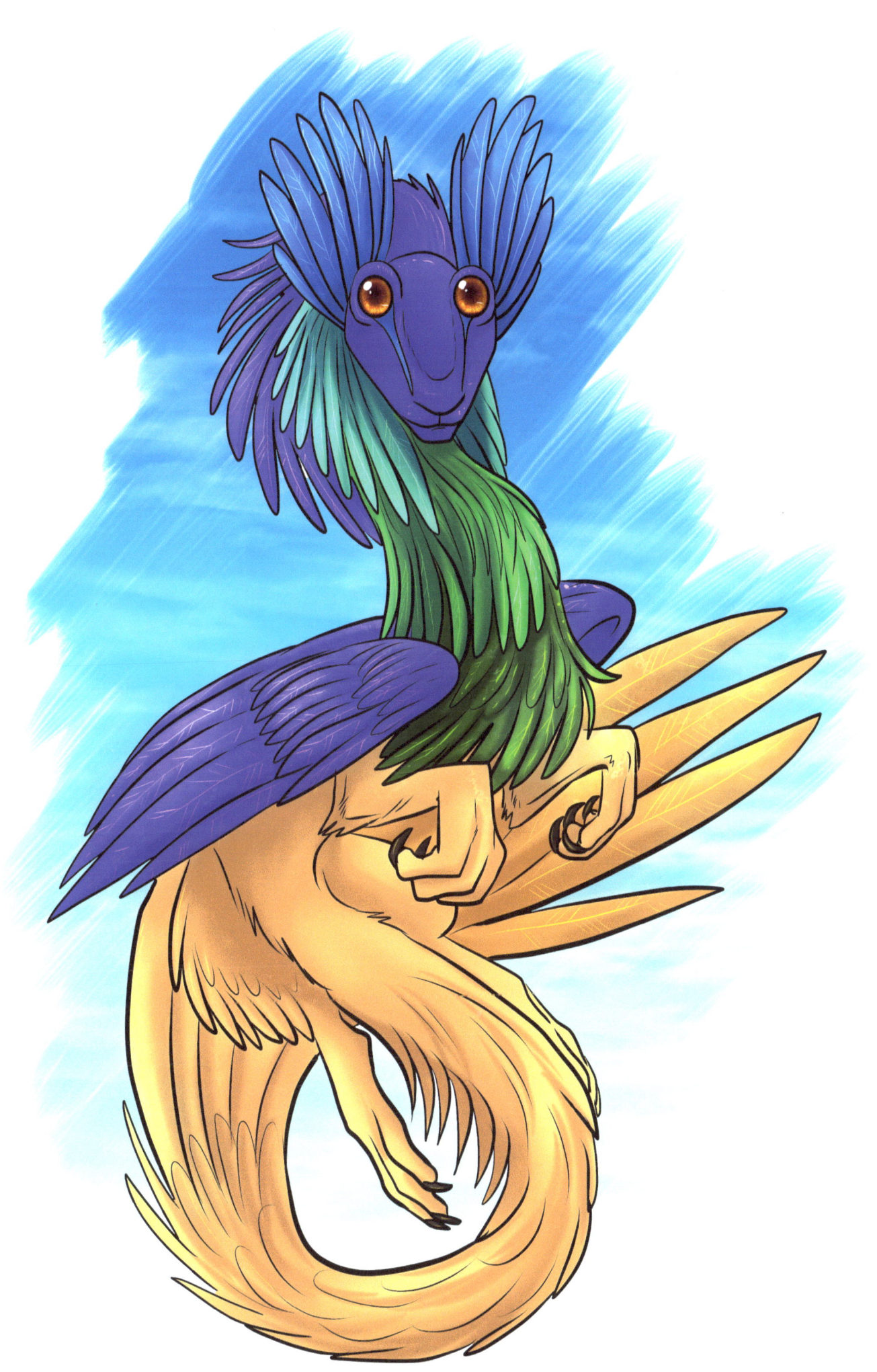

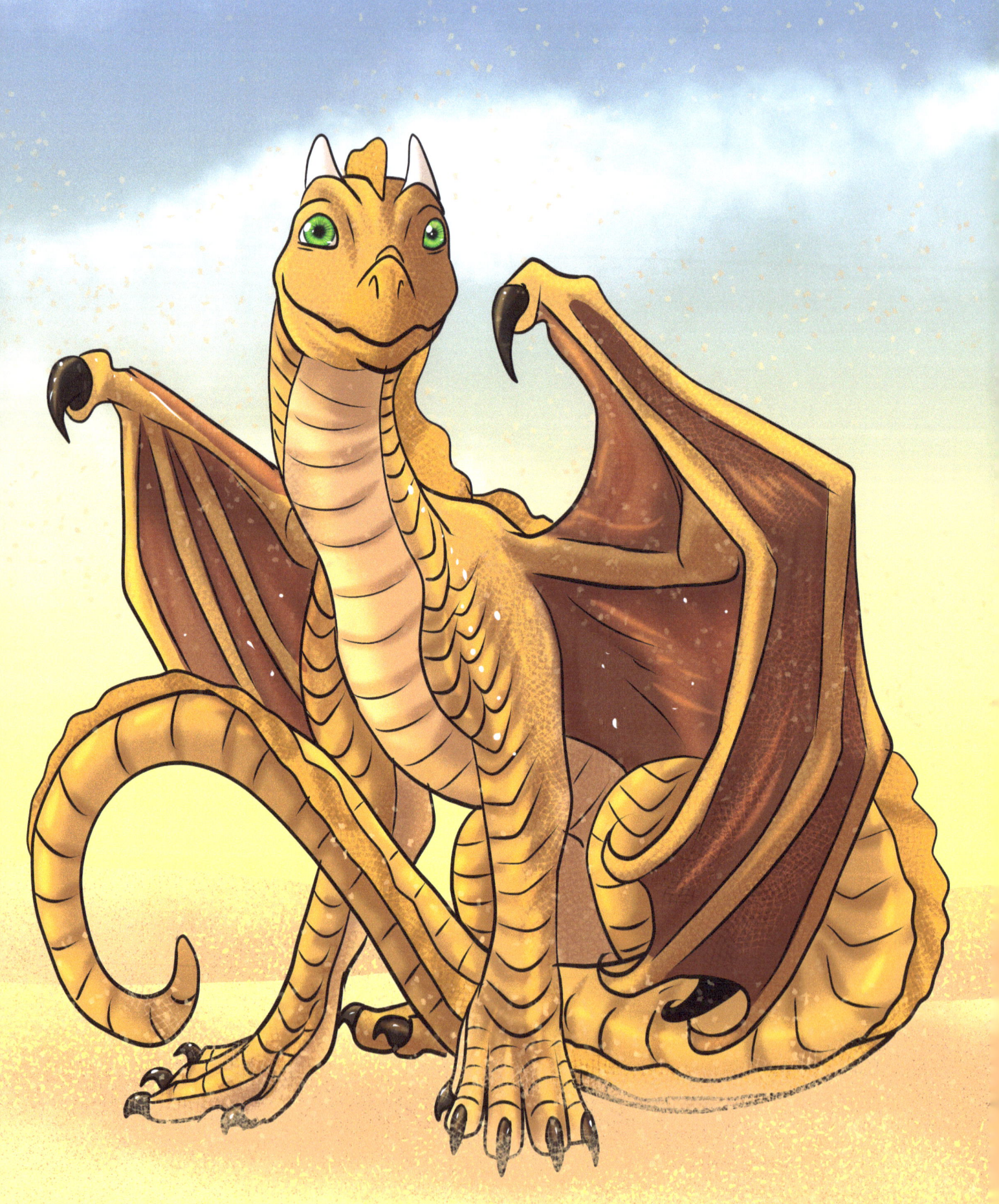

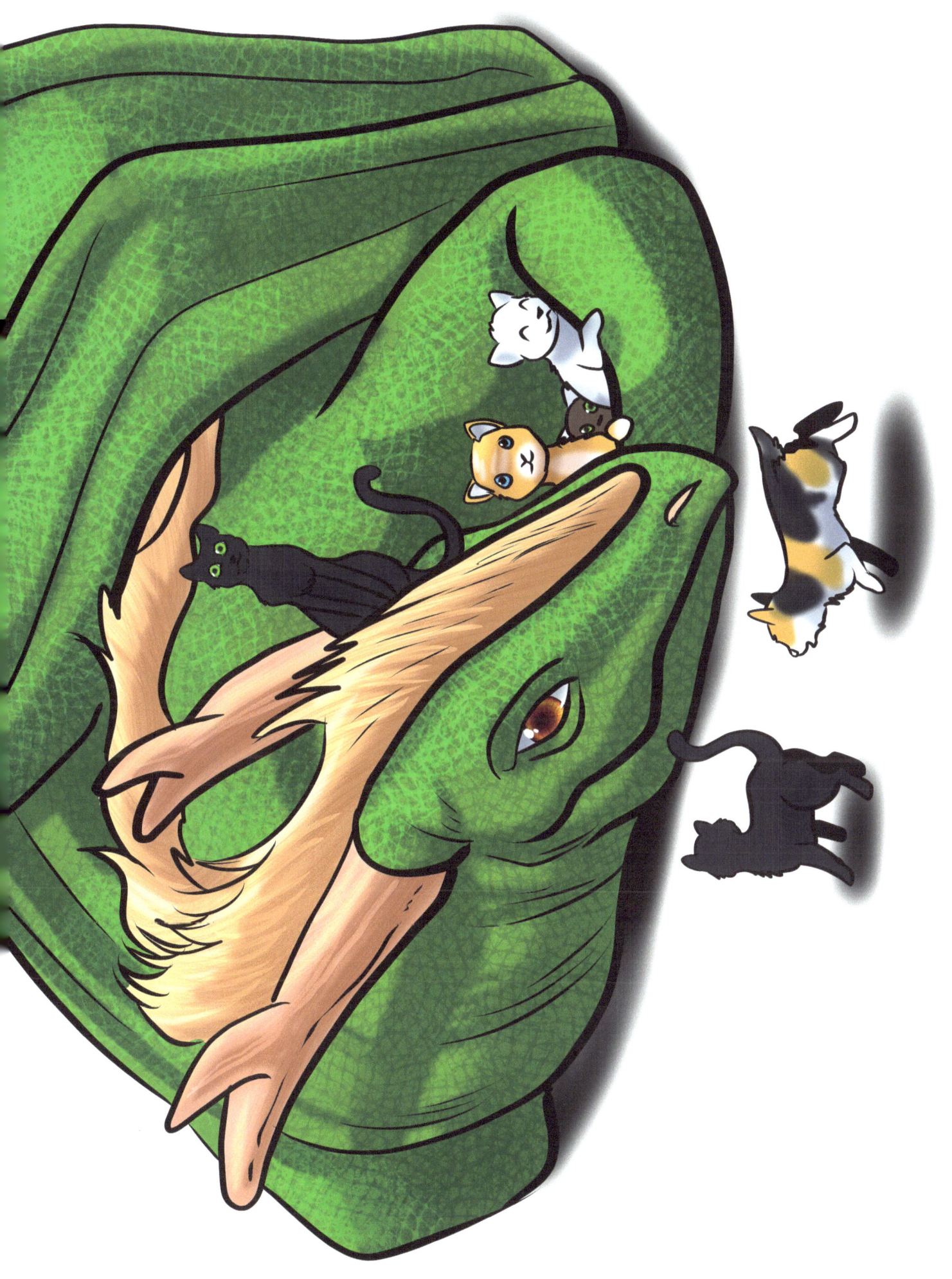

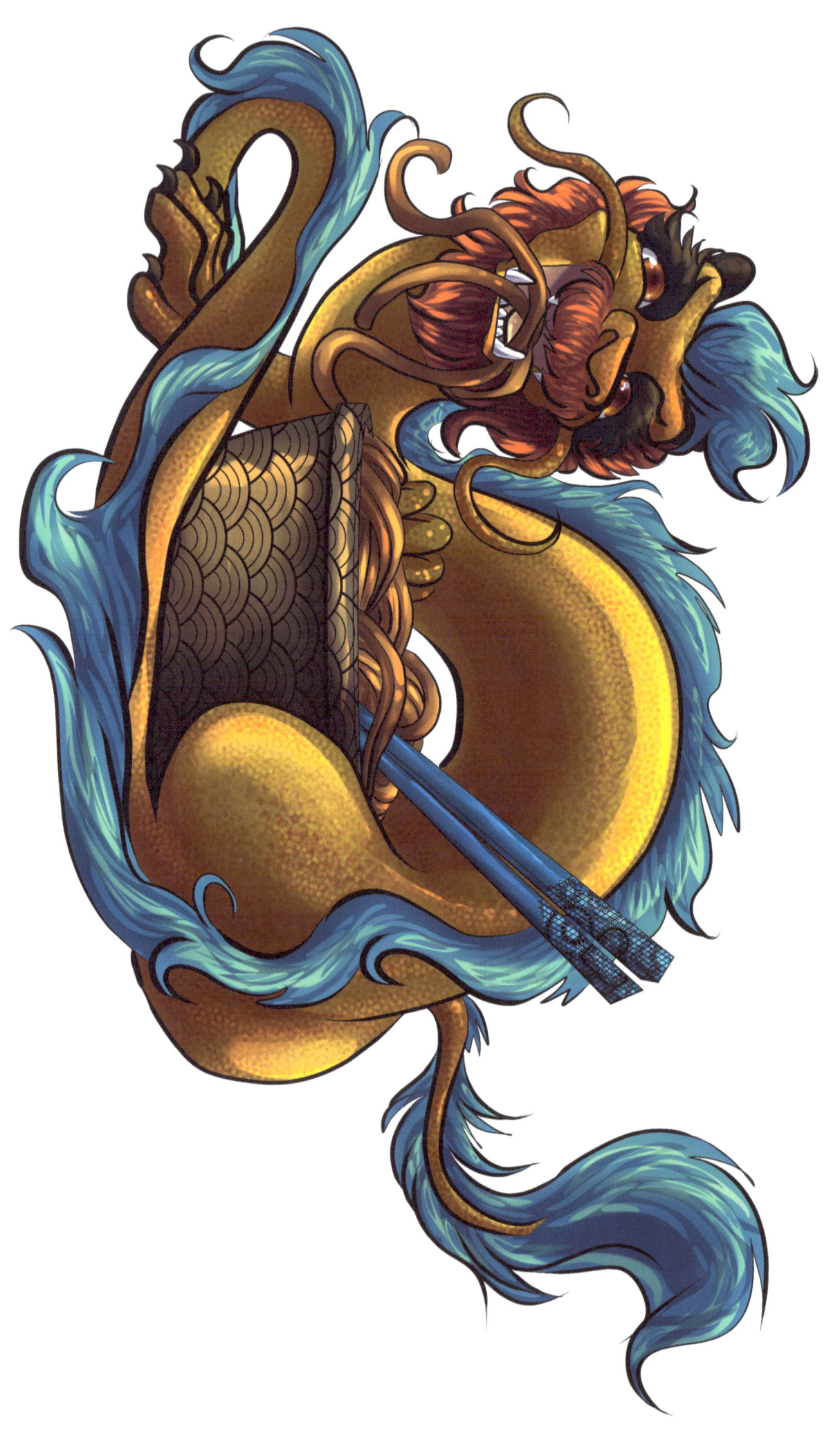

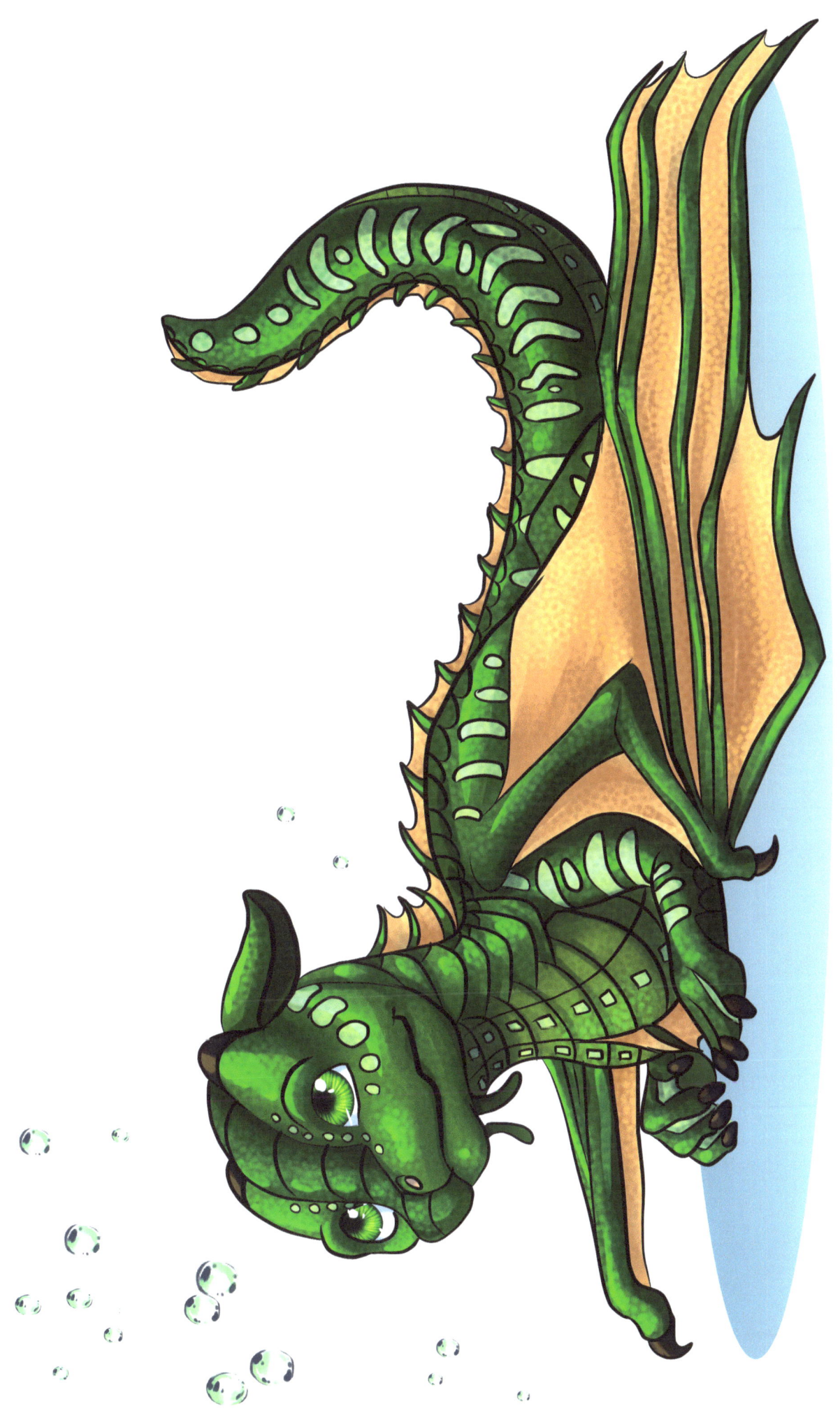

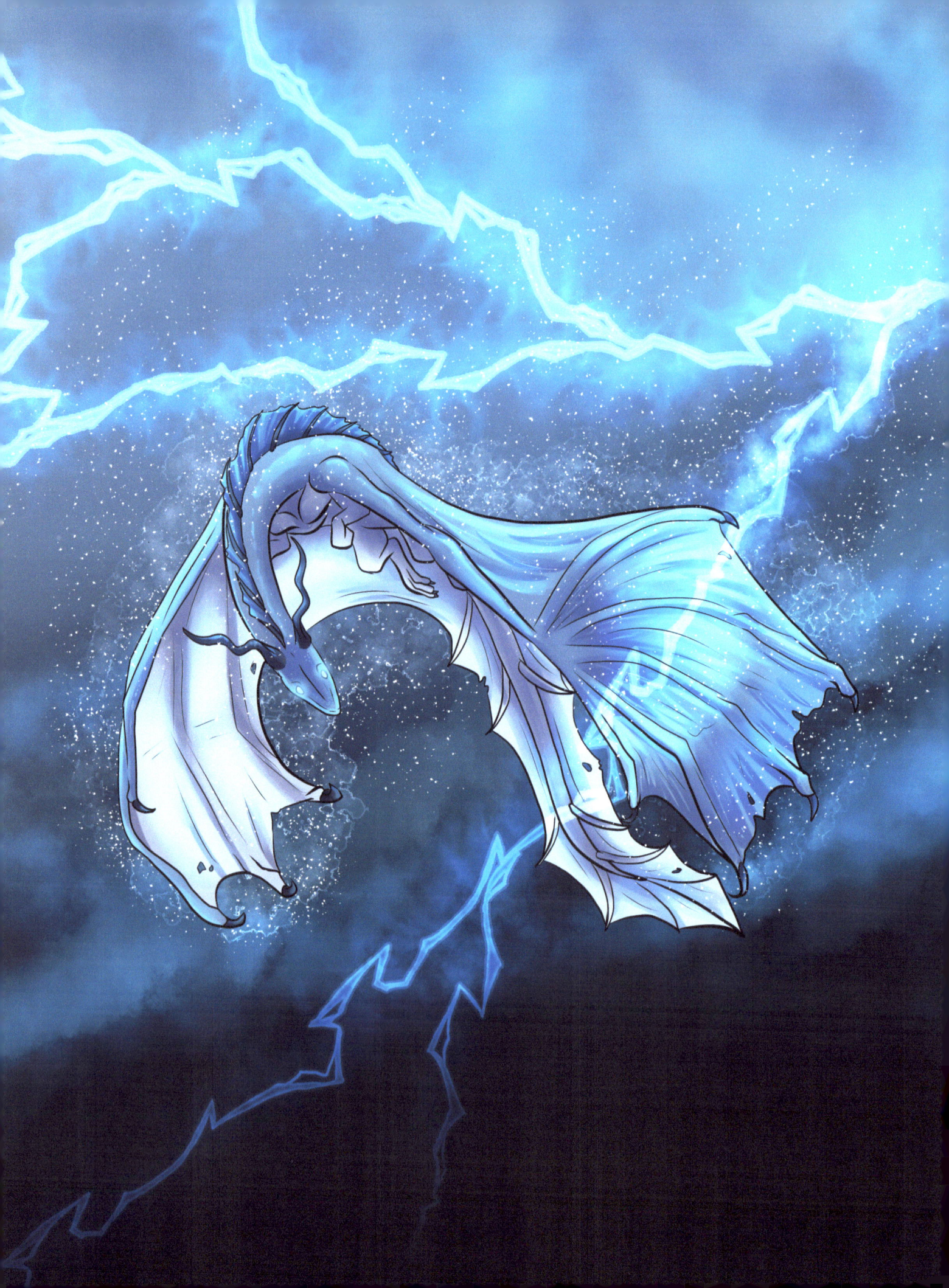

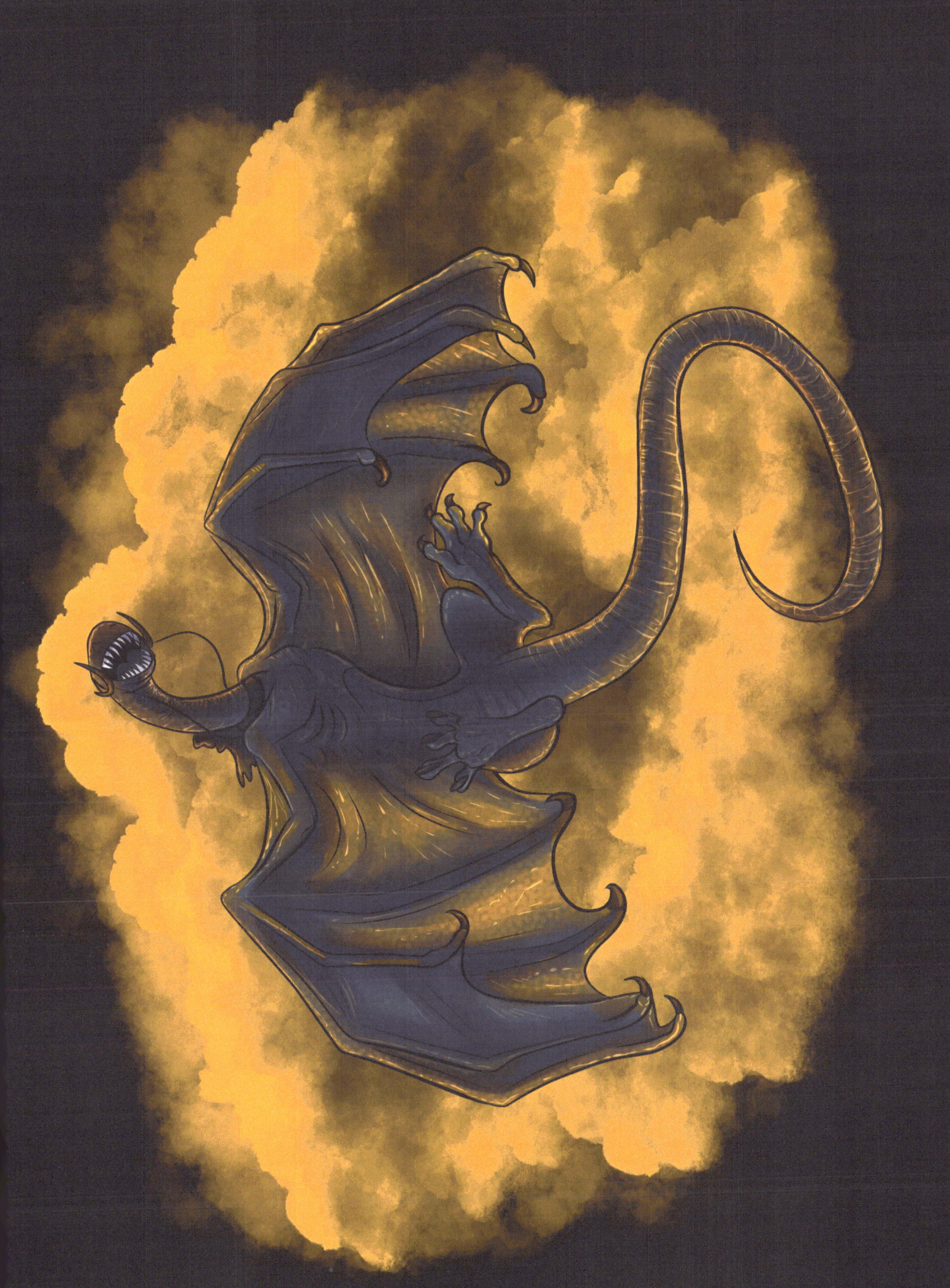

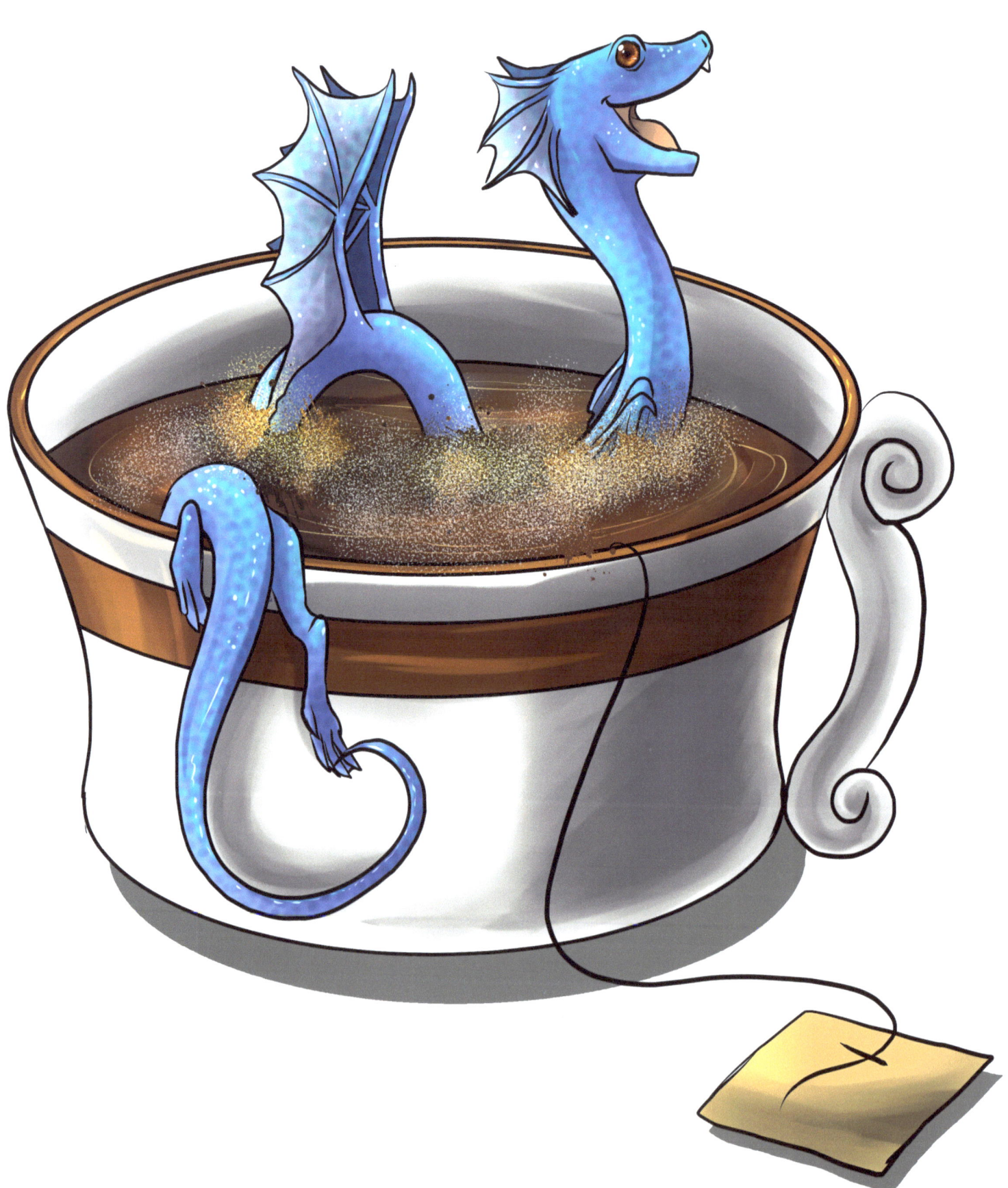

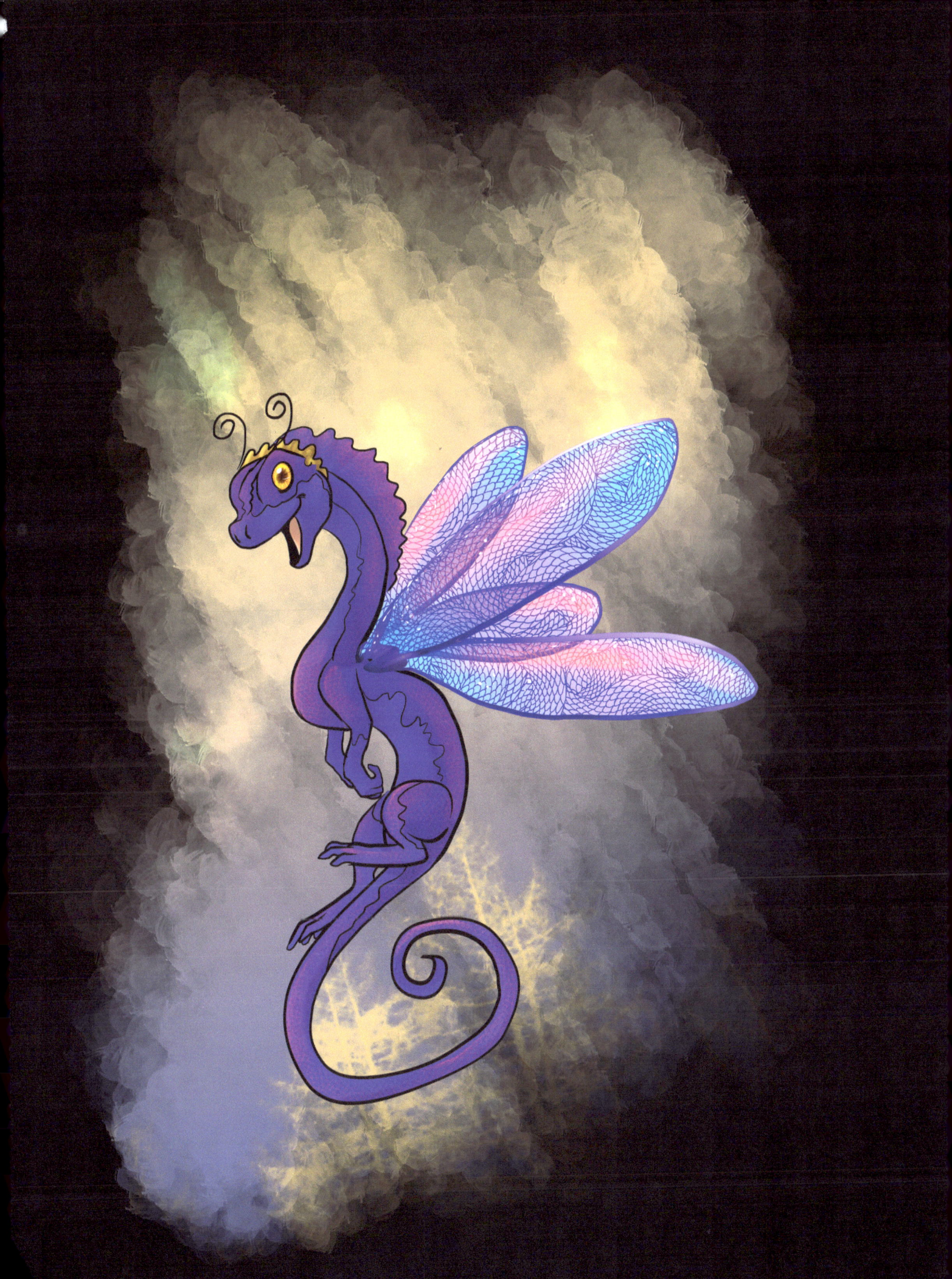

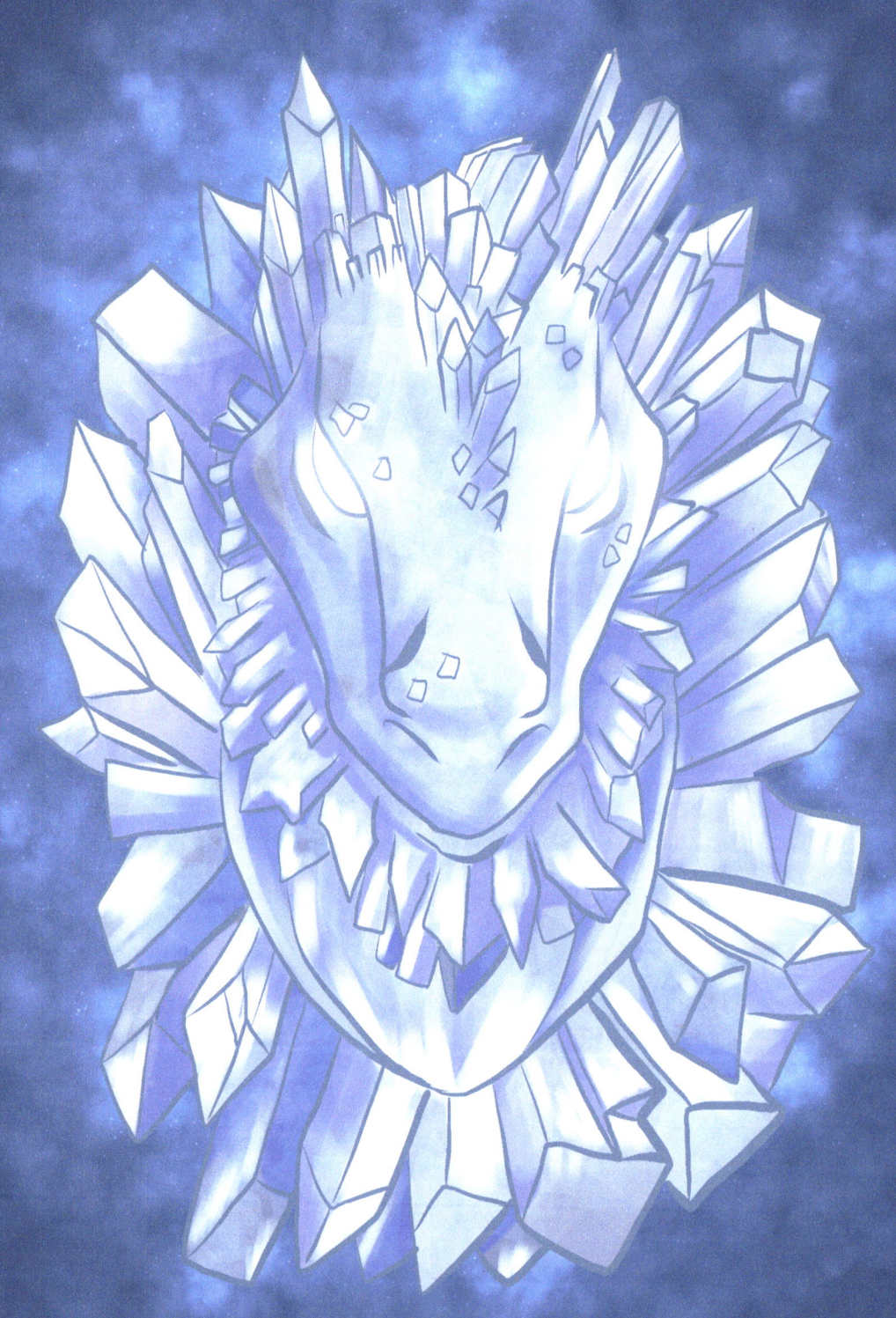

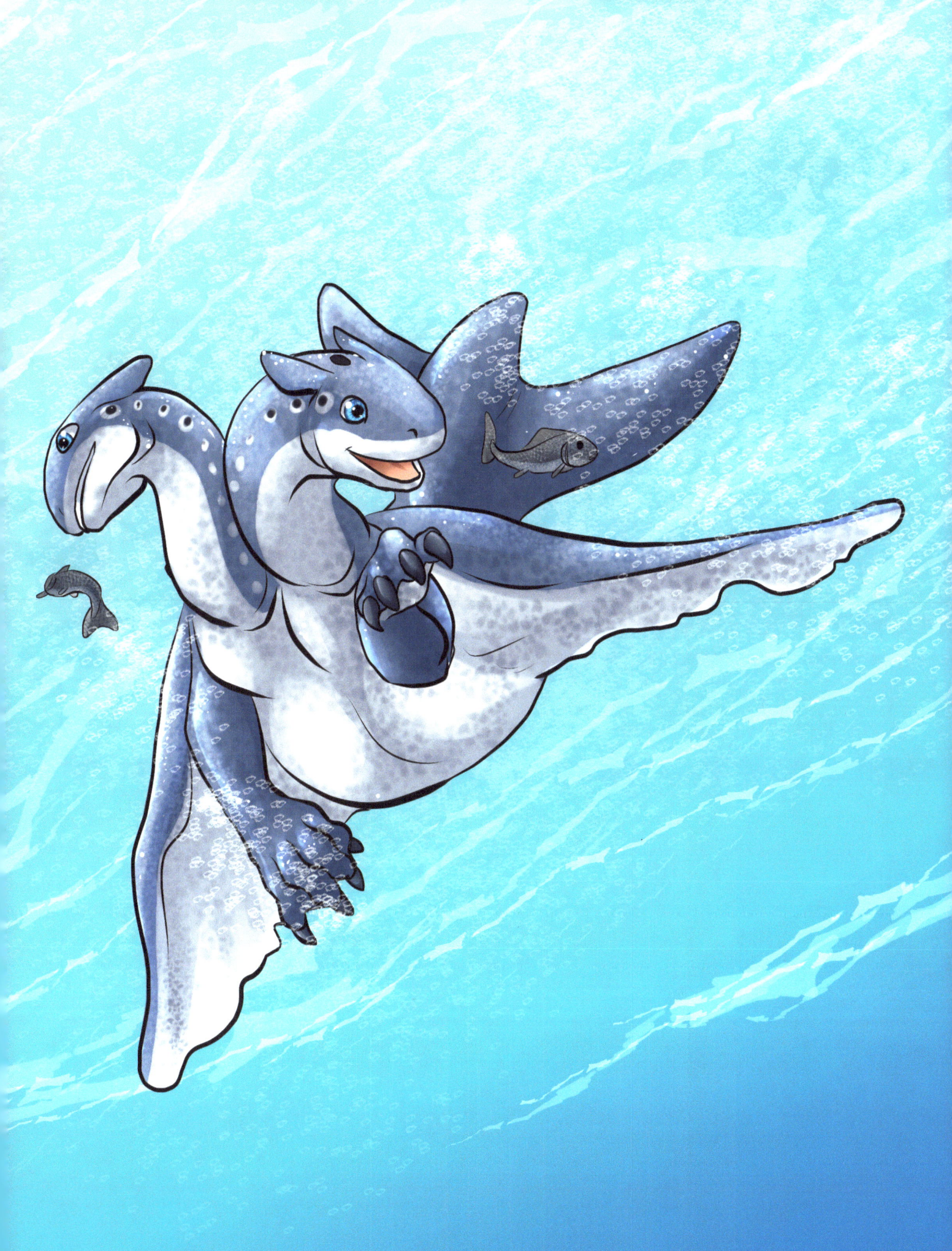

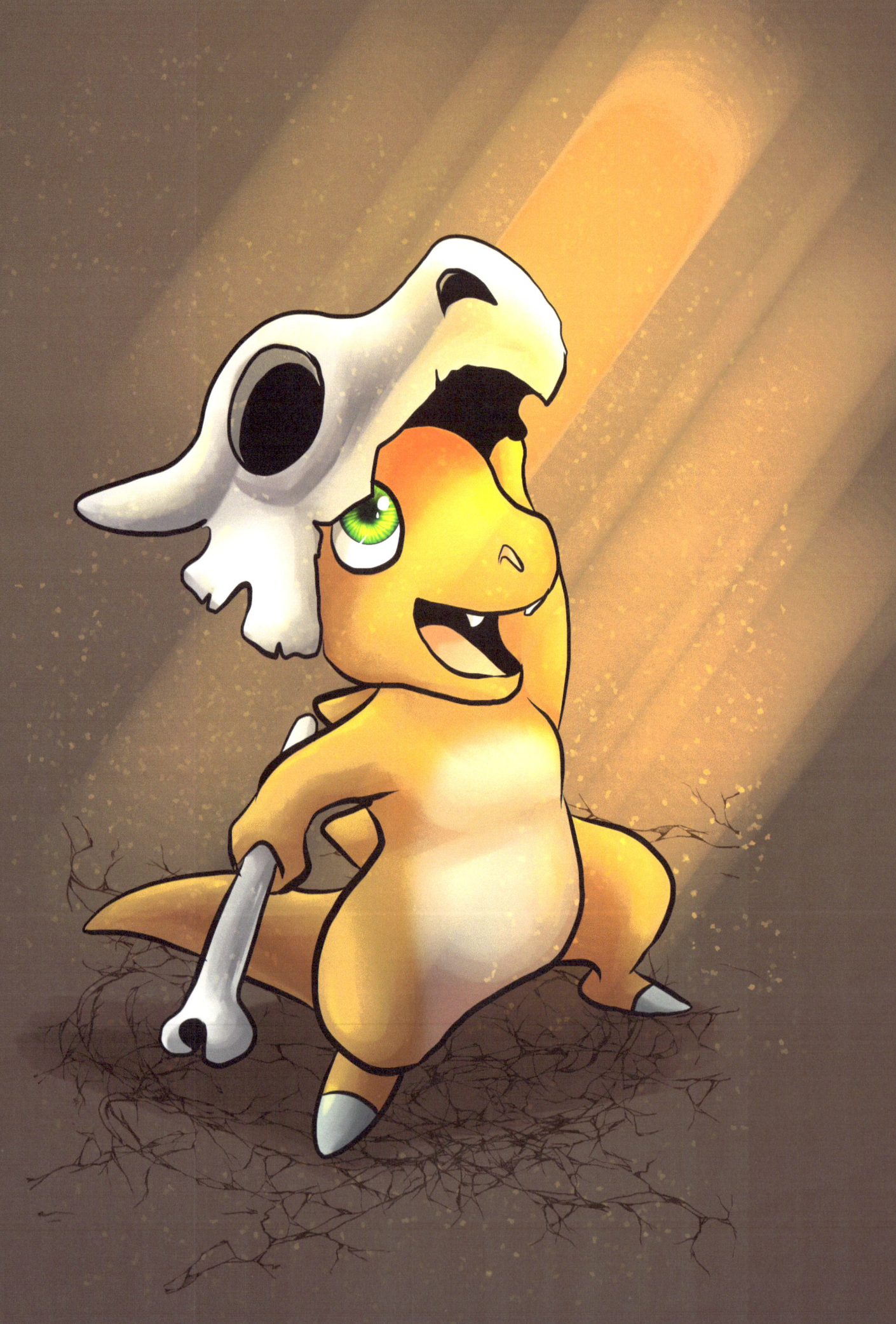

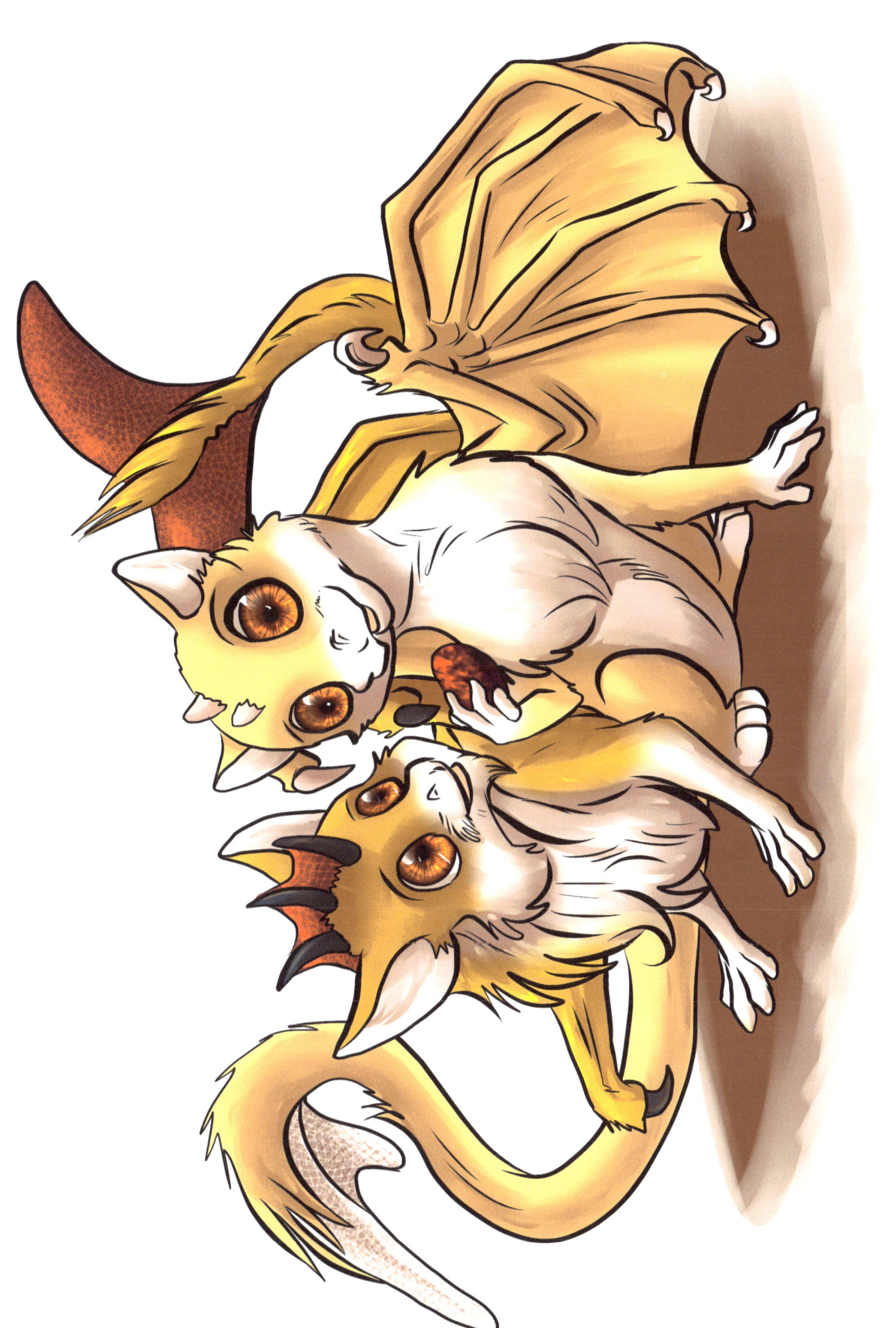

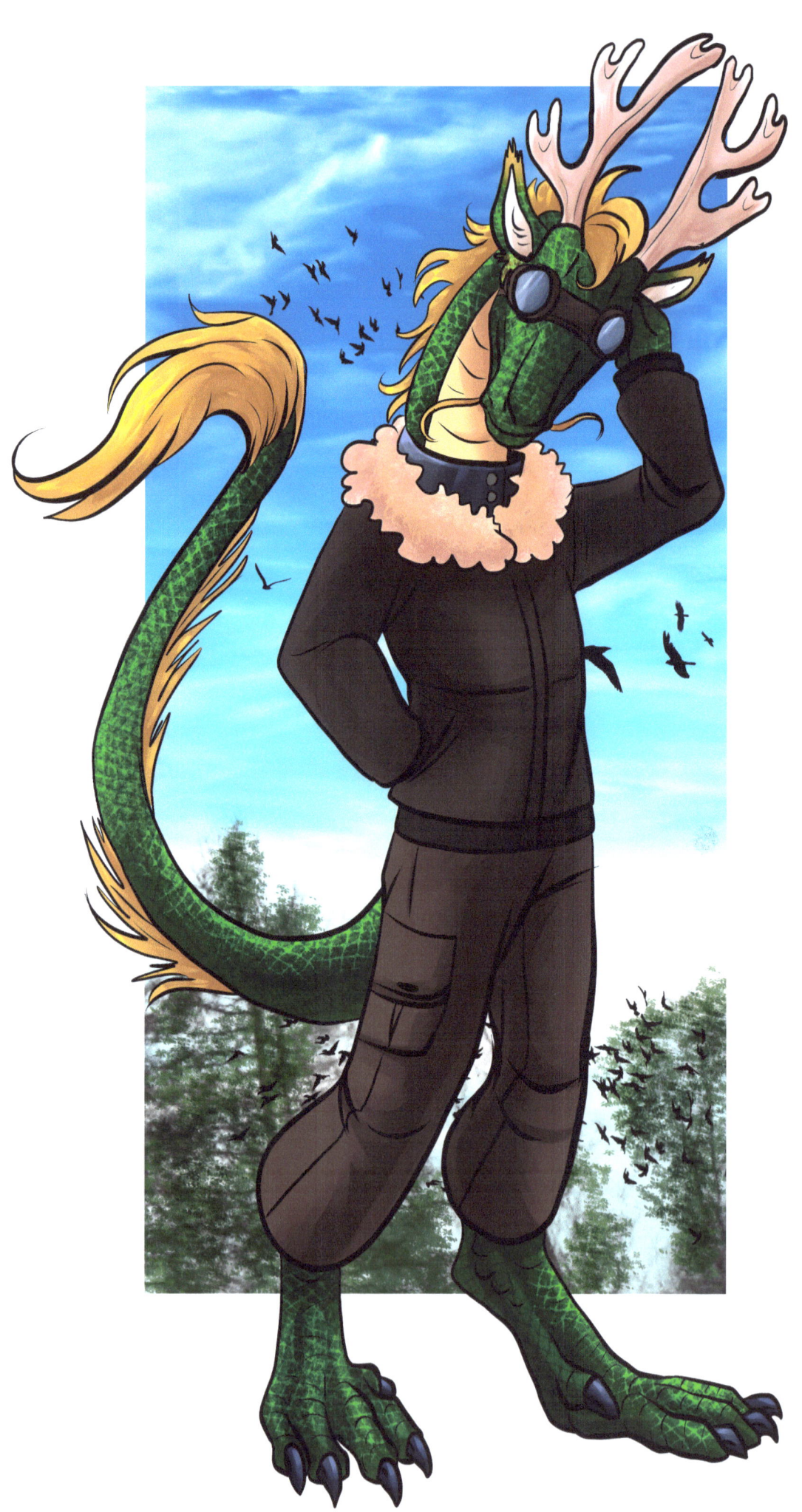

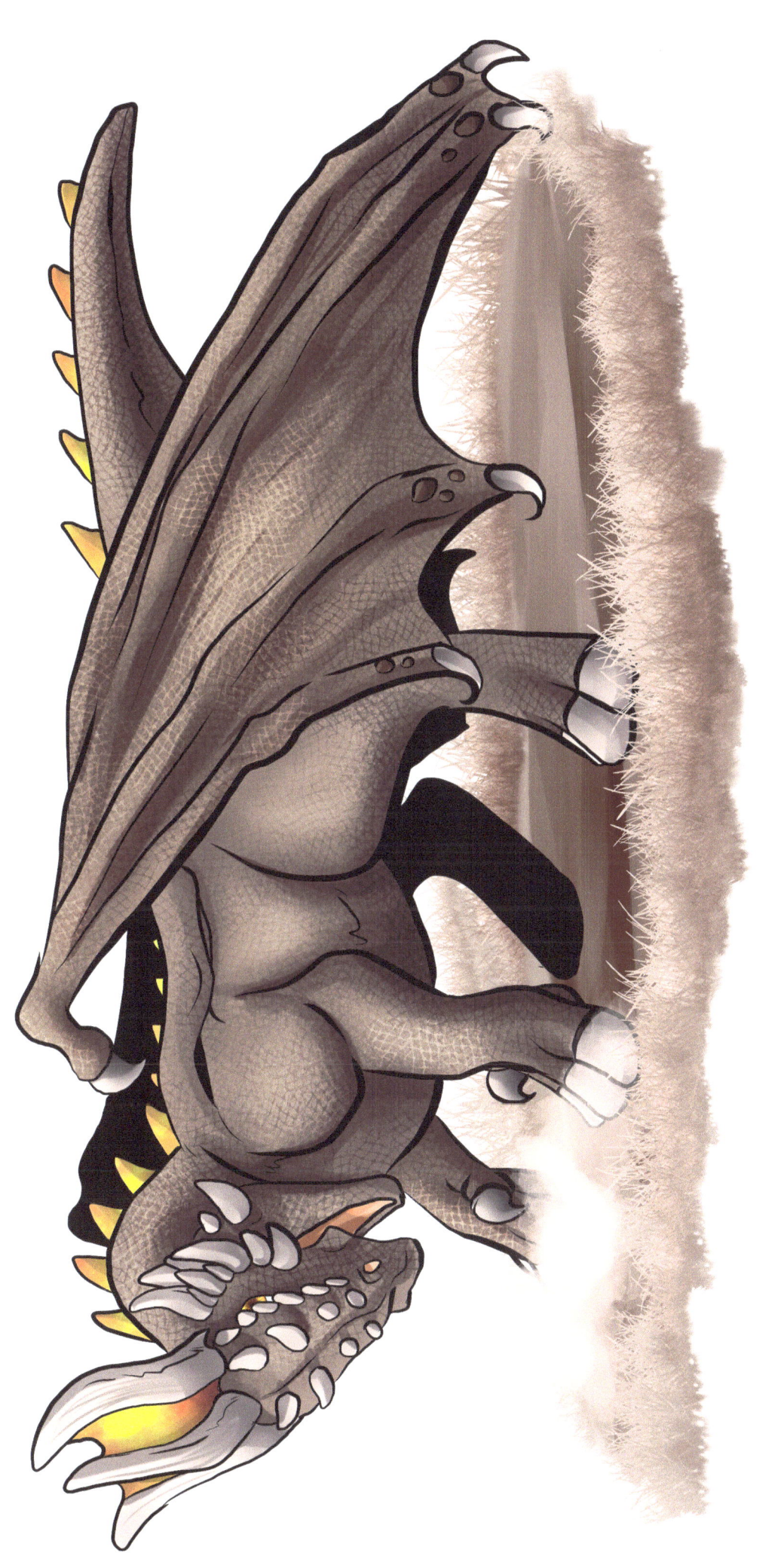

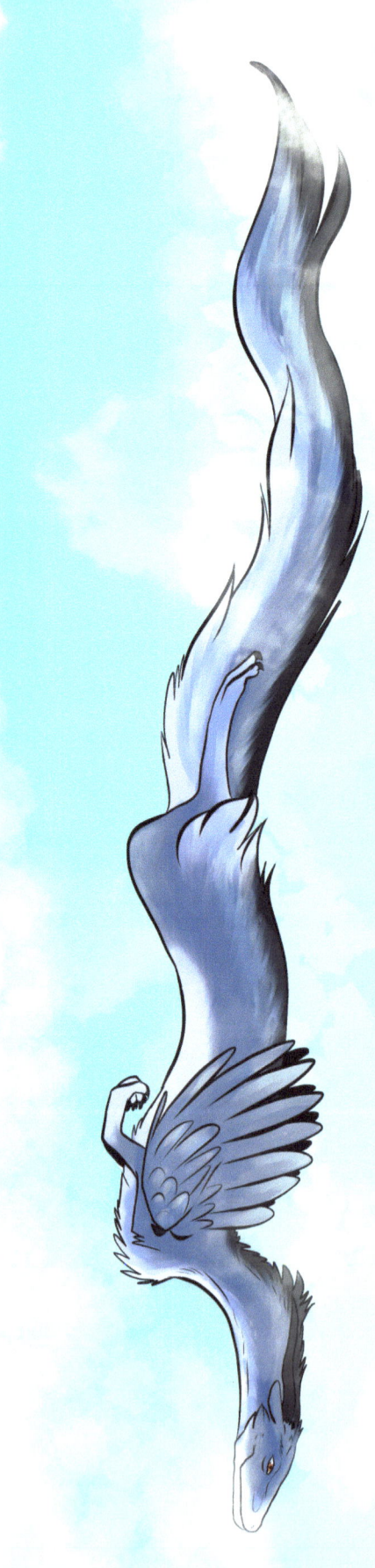

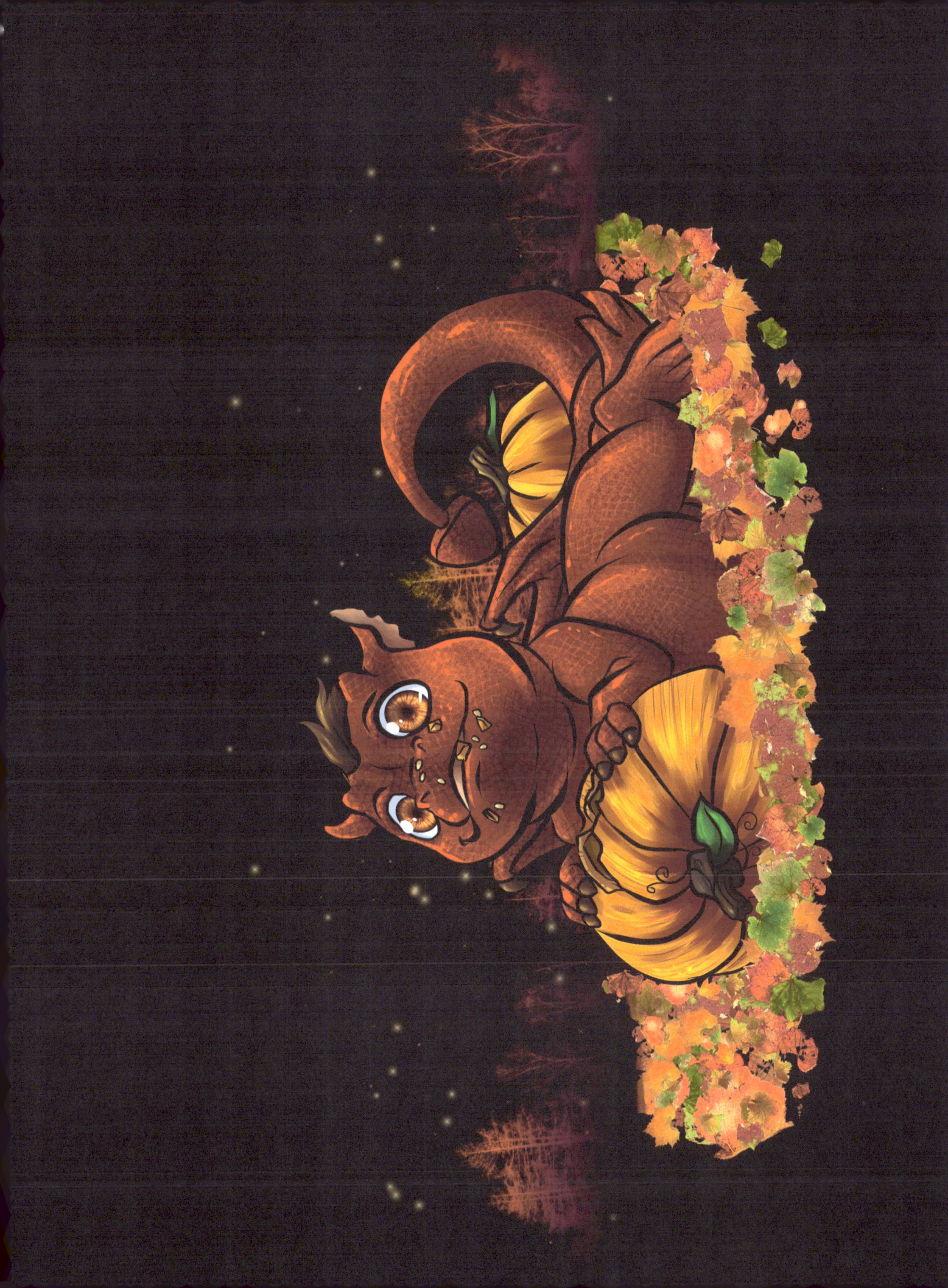

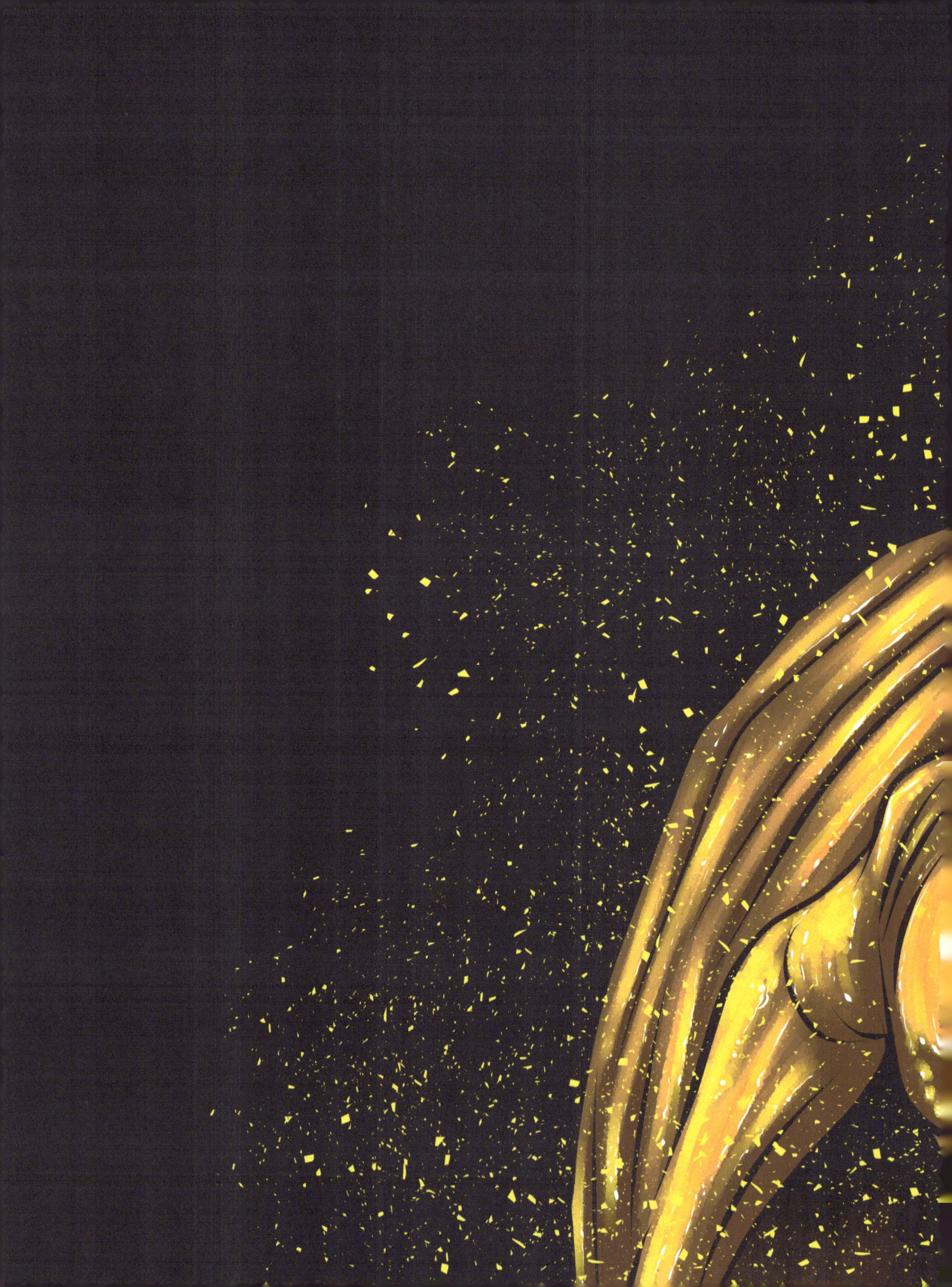

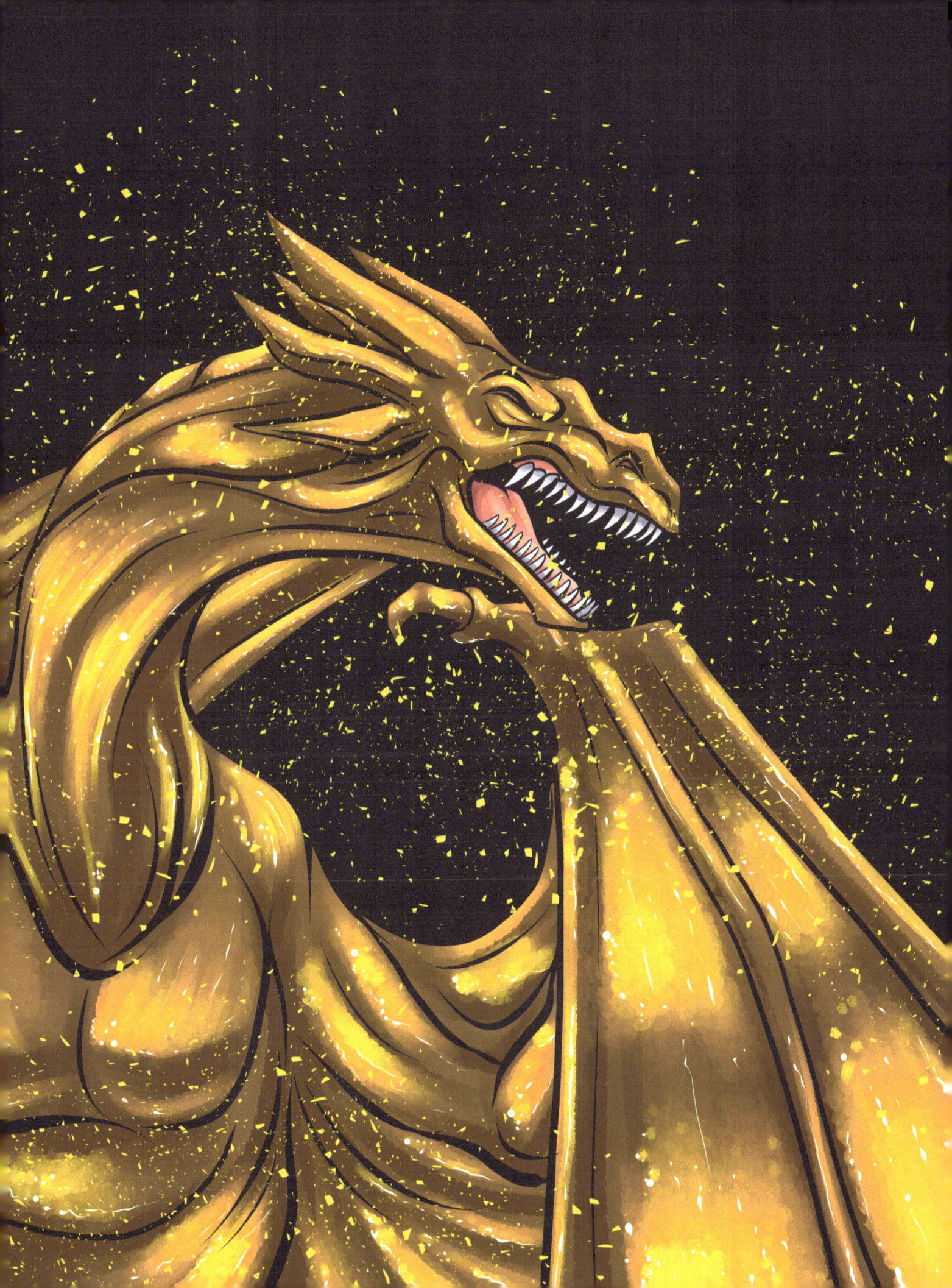

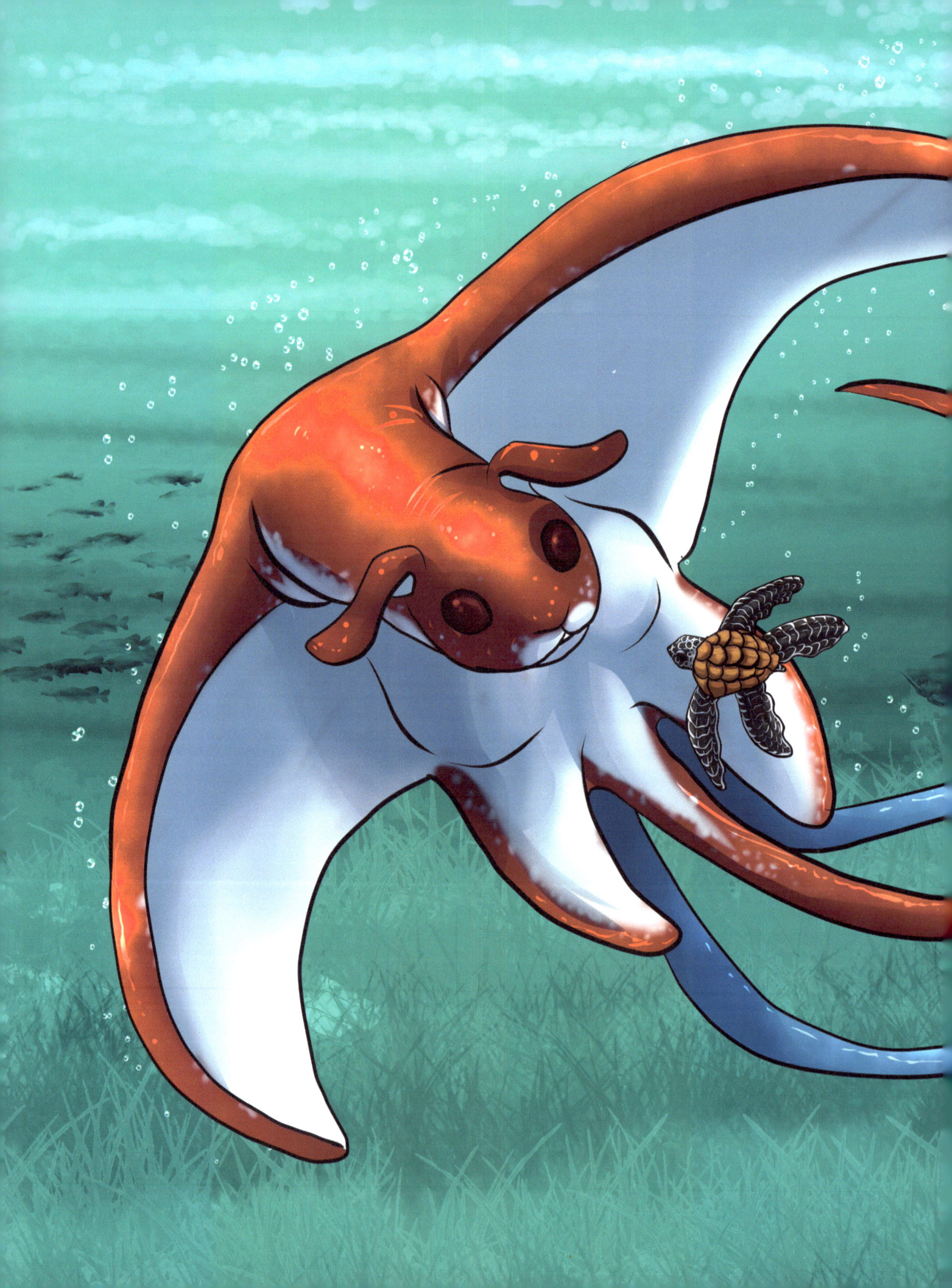

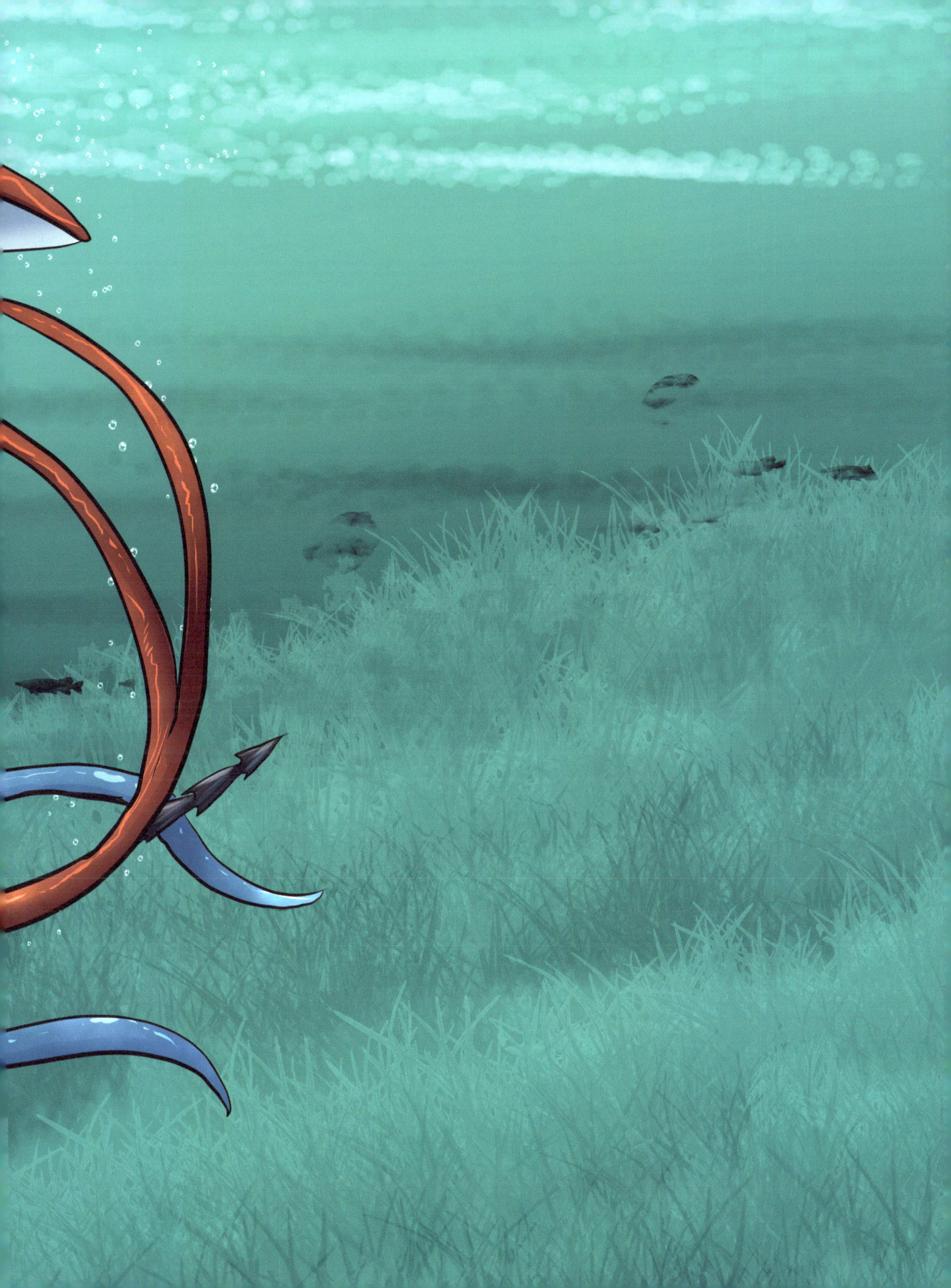

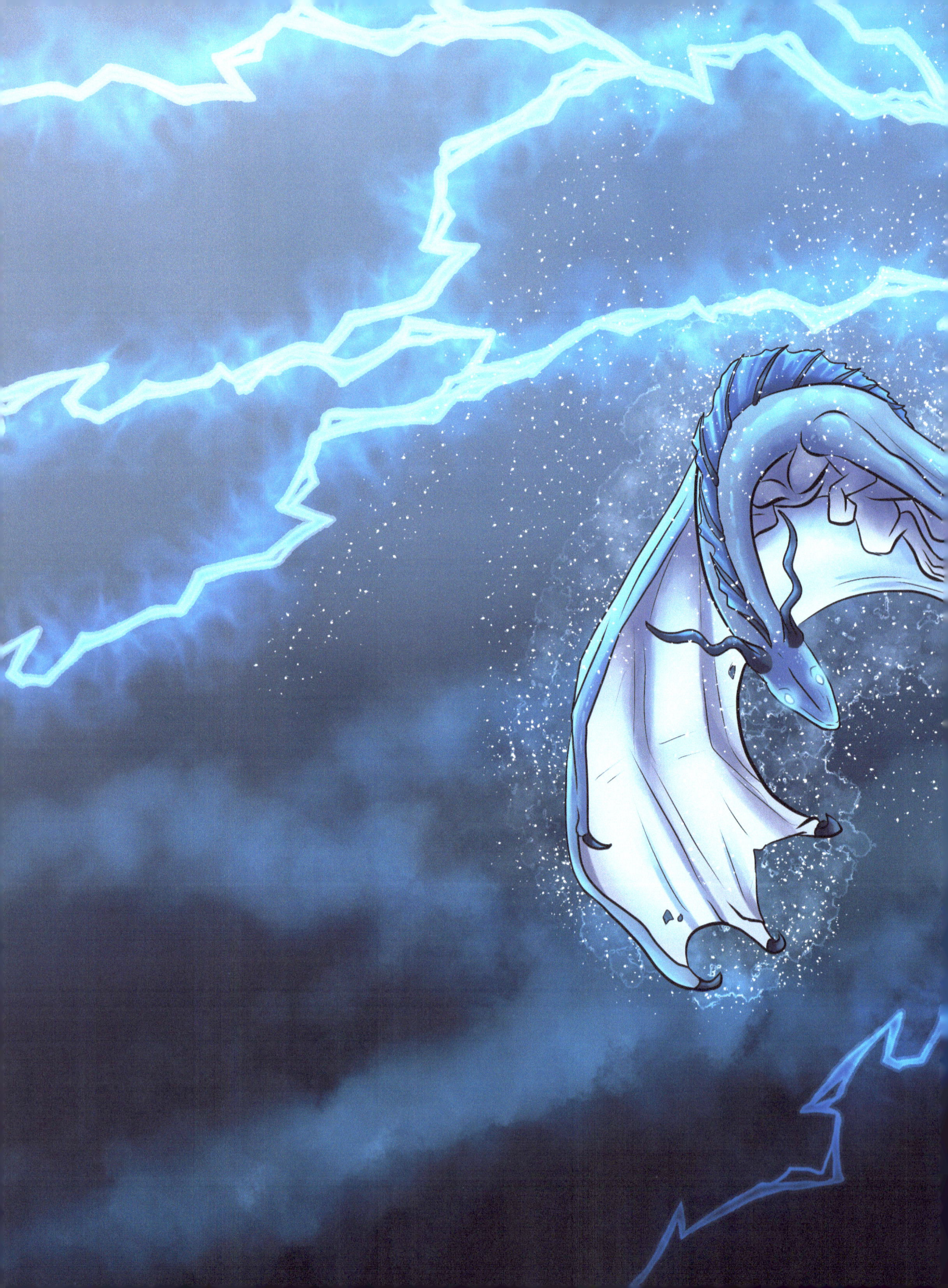

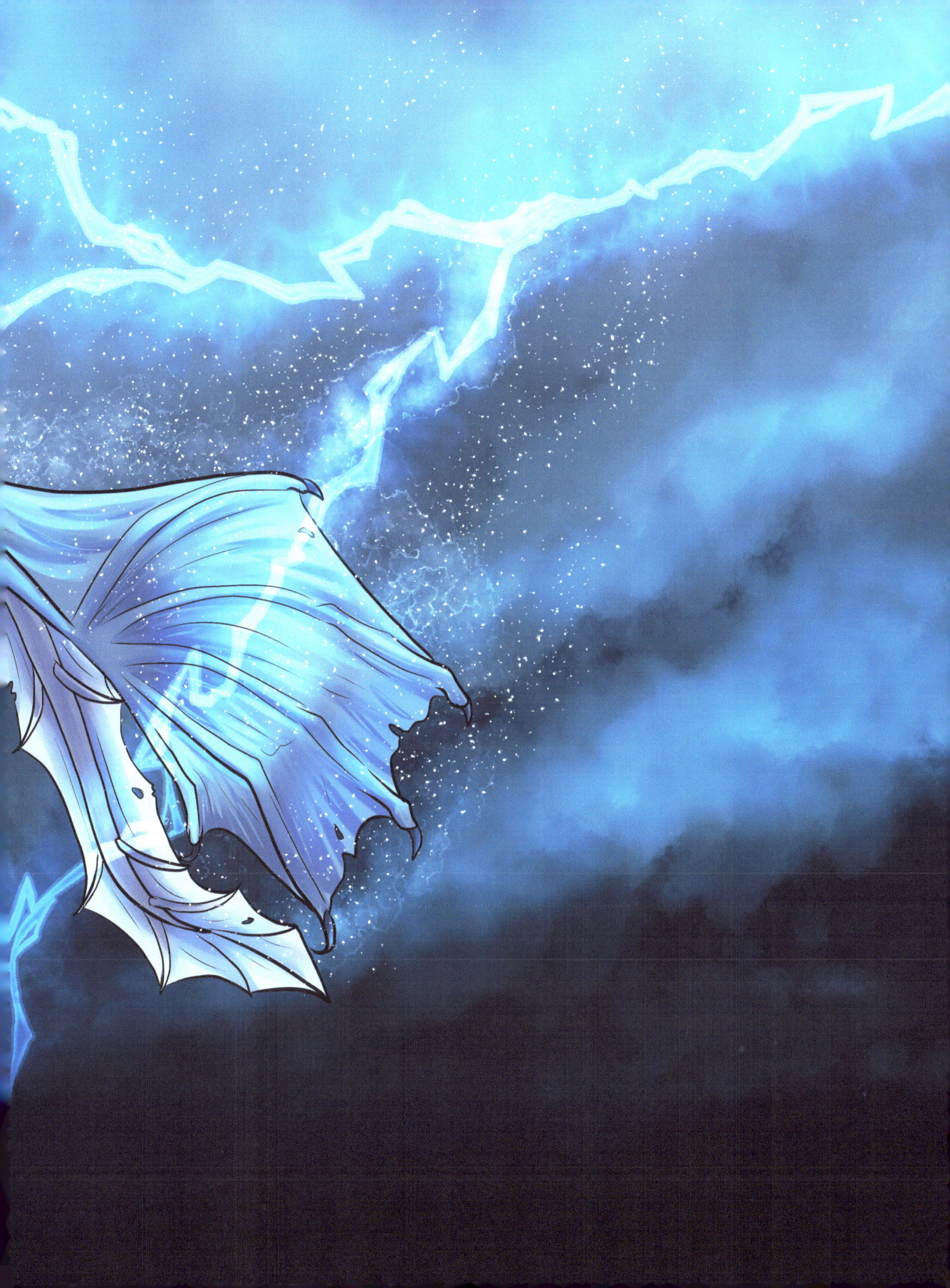

I HOPE YOU ENJOYED MY ART BOOK! YOU CAN BRING THIS BOOK TO MY TABLE AT CONVENTIONS AND GET A QUICK PENCIL SKETCH ON THIS PAGE OF A DRAGON!

FOR MORE OF MY ART, VISIT SHIVAE.NET!

www.ingramcontent.com/pod-product-compliance
Lightning Source LLC
Chambersburg PA
CBHW040447220526
45473CB00004B/1547